WORLD WAR II FROM ORIGINAL SOURCES

GERMAN
ANTI-PARTISAN COMBAT

EDITED AND INTRODUCED BY
BOB CARRUTHERS

Pen & Sword
MILITARY

This edition published in 2013 by
Pen & Sword Military
An imprint of
Pen & Sword Books Ltd
47 Church Street
Barnsley
South Yorkshire
S70 2AS

First published in Great Britain in 2012 in digital format by
Coda Books Ltd.

ISBN 978 1 78159 208 3

This book includes extracts from 'German Antiguerrilla Operations in the Balkans (1941-1944)' CMH Publication 104-18 published in 1953 by the Center of Military History, United States Army, Washington D.C., 'Rear Area Security in Russia - The Soviet Second Front Behind The German Lines' Department of the Army Pamphlet 20-240 published in 1951 by the Center of Military History, United States Army, Washington D.C., 'Small Unit Actions During the German Campaign in Russia' Department of the Army Pamphlet 20-269 published in 1953 by the Center of Military History, United States Army, Washington D.C., 'Russian Combat Methods in World War Two' published in 1950 by the Center of Military History, United States Army, Washington D.C

A CIP catalogue record for this book is
available from the British Library

Printed and bound by CPI Group (UK) Ltd, Croydon, CR0 4YY

Pen & Sword Books Ltd incorporates the Imprints of Pen & Sword Aviation, Pen & Sword Family History, Pen & Sword Maritime, Pen & Sword Military, Pen & Sword Discovery, Pen & Sword Politics, Pen & Sword Atlas, Pen & Sword Archaeology, Wharncliffe Local History, Wharncliffe True Crime, Wharncliffe Transport, Pen & Sword Select, Pen & Sword Military Classics, Leo Cooper, The Praetorian Press, Claymore Press, Remember When, Seaforth Publishing and Frontline Publishing

For a complete list of Pen & Sword titles please contact
PEN & SWORD BOOKS LIMITED
47 Church Street, Barnsley, South Yorkshire, S70 2AS, England
E-mail: enquiries@pen-and-sword.co.uk
Website: www.pen-and-sword.co.uk

CONTENTS

FOREWORD

MUCH of what you are about to read here was originally published by the Center of Military History of the United States Army based in Washington, D.C. Out of print since the the fifties, it now forms part of the developing series entitled 'World War II From Original Sources'. The aim is to provide the reader with a varied range of materials drawn from original writings covering the strategic, operational and tactical aspects of the weapons and battles of Hitler's war. The concept behind the series is to provide the well-read and knowledgeable reader with access to long out of print sources to build a picture of a particular aspect of that titanic struggle.

I am pleased to report that the series has been well received and it is a pleasure to be able to bring these original sources back to new life and to the attention of an interested readership. I particularly enjoy re-discovering good sources like these , and I am pleased to be able to present them unadorned and unvarnished to a sophisticated audience. The readership I strive to serve is the increasingly well informed community of reader/historians which needs no editorial lead and can draw its own conclusions. I am well aware that our community is constantly striving to discover new nuggets of information, and I trust that with this volume I have managed to stimulate fresh enthusiasm and that at least some of these facts will be new to you and will provoke readers to research further down these lines of investigation, and perhaps cause established views to be challenged once more. I am aware at all times in compiling these materials that our relentless pursuit of more and better historical information is at the core our common passion. I trust that this selection will contribute to that search and will help all of us to better comprehend and understand the bewildering events of the last century.

In order to produce an interesting compilation giving a flavour of events at the strategic and operational level I have returned once more to the Centre Of Military History series, which contain an intriguing series of near contemporary reviews. I find this series particularly fascinating as they provide us with a sense of what was happening at the face of battle almost as the events unfolded. I have also drawn upon the extensive writings of Erhard Raus, a man who knew Russia like no other.

Thank you for buying this volume in the series we hope you will enjoy discovering some new insights you will go on to try the others in the series.

Bob Carruthers
Edinburgh 2012

GERMAN ANTIGUERRILLA OPERATIONS IN THE BALKANS (1941-1944)

FOREWORD

THE purpose of this study is to describe briefly the German campaign against the guerrillas in the Balkans during the period of the European Axis occupation, from the end of hostilities against Greece and Yugoslavia in April 1941 to the capture of Belgrade by the Soviet forces and the Partisans in October 1944. The activities of Germany's Italian, Bulgarian, Croatian, and other allies, as well as the British, Soviet, and United States forces in the area, are treated only to the extent that they affected German operations. In sequence of time, this study is a continuation of Department of the Army CMH Pub 104-18, The German Campaigns in the Balkans (Spring 1941), of November 1953.

The material for this study was obtained from German military records now in the custody of The Adjutant General, Department of the Army. In addition to these official records, monographs by former German officers who participated in these operations furnished considerable general information and were of assistance in supplementing the terse official reports of specific actions. The authors of these monographs, prepared for the Historical Division, United States Army, Europe, include General der Gebirgstruppen (Lieutenant General) Hubert Lanz, former commander of the XXII Mountain Corps, and Polizeioberst (Colonel of Police) Karl Gaisser, German technical adviser to the Croatian Police.

7

The work of preparing this study was done by Major Robert M. Kennedy of the Office of the Chief of Military History. In its presentation, every effort was made to give an accurate account of the protracted attempt by the German occupation forces to destroy their elusive guerrilla enemy in this secondary theater of war from 1941 through 1944.

PART ONE
THE BALKAN AREA AND ITS PEOPLES

THE term "Balkan" is derived from a Turkish word meaning "mountain." As used by the English-speaking nations, however, the word refers to that peninsula of southeastern Europe lying between the Black and Adriatic Seas and extending south to the Mediterranean. To the north, the geographic boundary is less definite, but is generally accepted as the area south of the line of the Danube and Sava, west along the Kupa River, whence an imaginary line is drawn to the Adriatic port of Fiume.

From north to south, the broad expanse of the Danube Basin give a way to the mountain ranges of Yugoslavia and Bulgaria. The remainder of the peninsula consists mainly of rugged mountains, broken occasionally by such features as the coastal lowlands of Albania, the area surrounding the Gulf of Salonika in Greece, and the lowlands of Turkish Thrace.

The Balkan peoples have been in contact with the inhabitants of Asia Minor, the Hungarian Plain, Central Europe, and the highly developed Mediterranean civilizations for thousands of years. Nevertheless it is still possible to distinguish such ethnic groupings as the Albanians, Serbs, Bulgars, Turks, Greeks, and Vlachs, the last a semi-nomadic race of herdsmen being absorbed gradually into the various national states into which the Balkan area is divided.

Occupied for centuries by Romans, Turks, Austrians, and Hungarians, the Balkan peoples were forced to adopt the methods of irregular warfare in the struggle against their oppressors. When not resisting foreign invaders, they battled one another or kept alive their fighting traditions in bitter blood feuds. The mountainous terrain of their peninsula, with few good roads or rail lines, hampered the countermeasures of regular forces and made possible sustained guerrilla operations.

CHAPTER 1
PHYSICAL GEOGRAPHY

I. Topography

The most important physical feature of the Balkans as a scene of military operations is its wild terrain. The brushy mountain country, craggy peaks, and roadless forest areas offer irregular troops numerous places to hide, opportunity to shift forces unseen even from the air, and locations for ambush.

To the west, the Dinaric Alps follow Yugoslavia's Adriatic coast in a southeasterly direction and bar access to the interior of the country. Although some coastal areas are fertile, the limestone composition of these mountains makes the hinterland a barren region incapable of supporting any considerable population. Deep gorges make transverse movement difficult, and there are only a few secondary roads and rail lines until the central Yugoslav uplands to the east are reached.

From the headwaters of the Drin River, the length of Albania to the port city of Valona, the mountains draw back from the coast, making for easier access to the interior, and assume a north-south direction. South of Valona, the mountains resume their southeasterly march and merge into the Greek Pindus. These latter extend to the Gulf of Corinth, reappearing on the southern side of the gulf in the Peloponnesus. Directly south of Greece proper is the large island of Crete, of considerable strategic importance. Other Greek islands dotting the Ionian and Aegean Seas are Corfu, Cephalonia, Zante, Rhodes, the Dodecanese, the Sporades, the Cyclades, Lemnos, and Khios. The central uplands, east of the mountain chain extending the length of the Balkan Peninsula, are fertile enough to support large centers of population and some industry. To the north, this region is drained by the Sava and Morava Rivers, flowing into the Danube; to the south, by the Vardar, wending its way through Macedonia to the Gulf of Salonika and the Aegean.

The eastern portion of the peninsula is bisected by the Balkan Mountains. To the north this area descends to the Danubian plain; to the south, to the steppe-like lands of Turkish Thrace.

II. Climate

With the exception of its coastal areas, the Balkan Peninsula has a central European climate, characterized by warm and rainy summers and cold winters, differing little from the Danubian lands to the north. The Dalmatian coast of Yugoslavia, facing the Adriatic, and the Ionian ;and western Aegean coasts of Greece enjoy variations of the Mediterranean type of climate, with warm, dry summers and mild, rainy winter seasons; other coastal areas have a climate between that of central Europe and the Mediterranean-for example, the north Aegean coast with its hot summers and cold winters and the Black Sea coast with its moderately hot summers and cold winters.

CHAPTER 2

NATIONAL STATES

I. General

The peace treaties following the Balkan Wars of 1912 and 1913, World War I, and the Greek-Turkish conflict ending in 1923 resolved the frontiers of the various Balkan states until 1939. In that year, Italy occupied Albania and proceeded to implement her designs for dominating the Balkan Peninsula.

The creation of these states had satisfied many national aspirations, but numerous minority and territorial problems were left unsettled, and both Italians and Germans were able to turn them to their own advantage. Among the dissatisfied were the Hungarians in the part of north central Yugoslavia that had once been part of the Austro-Hungarian Empire; the Italians along Yugoslavia's northwestern border; the Macedonians, torn among the Bulgarians, Yugoslavs, and Greeks; and the large colonies of Austrians and Germans in northern Yugoslavia. There were also bitter rivalries between member nations of the same state, as the Serbs and Croats of Yugoslavia, and both Yugoslavia and Bulgaria were resentful of Greek possession of the Aegean coast. Despite the efforts of some Balkan leaders to foster intra-Balkan cooperation and good will prior to 1941, these sources of animosity and friction remained to hamper resistance to Italian and German subjugation.

II. Greece

Slightly smaller in area than England, Greece had a population of less than eight million in 1941. Migrations and exchanges of population, chief among them the replacement of Turks in western Thrace with a million and a quarter Greeks expelled from Asia Minor in 1922-24, contributed to making the inhabitants of the Hellenic state predominantly Greek by the outbreak of World War II. Although there were a number of Albanians and Vlachs in the Pindus Mountains area, they presented no minority problem.

Athens, the capital, with its port city of Piraeus, was the nucleus of the Greek maritime system; Salonika was a center of land transportation and an important seaport for the more northerly of the Balkan countries. With an economy based chiefly on ocean commerce and processing of goods mainly to olive oil, currants, and tobacco. Cereals led among heavy food imports, since Greece could not feed its own population on its domestic production. When Italian forces attacked from occupied Albania on 28 October 1940, the Greeks adopted a strategy of holding lightly on their left, allowing Italian columns to advance deep into the barren Pindus, while they resisted strongly and then launched a counteroffensive on their right. Their advance brought the Greeks into Albania, where they presented a serious threat to the left flank of the Italian forces to the south. Despite their victories over the Italian invaders, the Greeks could not long resist the fast-moving German forces that intervened in the Greek-Italian conflict on 6 April 1941. Greece surrendered to the Germans on 23 April, and was then required to surrender to the Italians as well. This submission to an enemy they had all but defeated aroused the resentment of the Greeks. Later coupled with the occupation of most of Greece by Italian forces, it contributed in no small measure to the rise of the Greek resistance movement.

III. Yugoslavia

A most heterogeneous state, the homeland of the Serbs, Croats, and Slovenes, derived its name from the Slavic terms for South Slav and became a state following World War I. Yugoslavia had a population of nearly sixteen millions by 1941, and in geographic area was slightly smaller than the state of Wyoming.

Sixteen blindfolded partisan youth await execution by German forces in Smederevska Palanka, Serbia. Executed with this group was a German soldier, who refused to take part in the action, 20 August 1941

Almost one half of its inhabitants, or six and one-half million people, were Serbs, occupying the areas of the former Kingdom of Serbia and the old provinces of Bosnia, Herzegovina, and Dalmatia. The Serbs used the Cyrillic alphabet, professed mainly the Orthodox faith though many Serbs were Moslems, and stubbornly resisted the Central Powers in World War I. Serbian Belgrade was the seat of the Yugoslav national government, lending credence to the claim of the minorities that the Serbs dominated the state. It was the Serbs' violent protest to Regent Paul's accord with Hitler and their overthrow of the government in March 1941 that precipitated the German attack the following month, and it was from among the Serbs that the Chetniks rose to resist the occupation forces. Next in numbers to the Serbs were the Croats, some three and three-quarter million, inhabiting the northwestern part of Yugoslavia. The traditional capital of the Croats was Zagreb, and their territory was part of the Austro-Hungarian Empire until the end of World War I. The Croats were culturally more advanced than the Serbs, were western European in their outlook, and the majority professed Catholicism. Although their language was related closely to that of the Serbs, the Croats used the Latin alphabet. German influence among the Croats in the pre-1941 period was strong, and it was on the traditional Croatian hostility to the Serbs that the invaders placed much confidence in 1941.

Last among the major racial groups comprising the Yugoslav state were the Slovenes, inhabiting the most northerly portion of the country and numbering some one and one-half million. Like the Croats, the Slovenes were culturally well advanced, used the Latin alphabet, were oriented toward the West, and for the most part Catholic. Their historic capital was Ljubljana, and the German influence was very marked.

Smaller national minorities included one-half million Hungarians and almost as many Albanians; one-quarter million Romanians; and splinter groups of Czechs, Slovaks, and other Slavic peoples. There were also well over one-half million Austrians and Germans. In 1941 over three quarters of the Yugoslav population worked the land, and agriculture formed the nation's economic base. The chief exports were lumber, bauxite, copper, some iron ore, and processed fruits; imports included textiles and machinery. Deposits of iron ore near the surface of the ground could not be used to build up a sizable steel industry because of the shortage of coking coal.

The German onslaught of 6 April 1941 caught the Yugoslavs in the midst of general mobilization, a measure that had been delayed to avoid giving provocation to Hitler. A devastating air attack on Belgrade the day hostilities commenced crippled communications between the Yugoslav High Command and the armies in the field. To placate the dissatisfied minorities, which charged that the Serb dominated government would defend only Serb-inhabited areas, the Yugoslav Army was deployed all around the borders of the country. To make the Yugoslav position even more difficult, thousands of Croat reservists did not report as directed for military service. By 17 April the German Second Army from the northwest and the Twelfth Army from the southeast, assisted to some extent by their Italian allies, had broken through the thin shell of resistance around the country, captured all major cities, and forced the Yugoslav High Command to capitulate.

IV. Albania

This smallest of the Balkan countries, approximately the size of Maryland, had a population of slightly over one million in 1941. After centuries of Turkish domination, Albania had declared its independence in 1912, but it was not until the end of World War I that the tiny state could consider itself free of its stronger neighbors. Consisting mainly of Gheg tribesmen in the north and Tosks in the south, the Albanians were almost exclusively an agricultural and stock-raising people. Mineral and lumber resources were largely undeveloped because of a lack of transportation, although the Italians managed to produce some oil and completed part of the short rail line from Tirana to the Adriatic after their occupation of the country in 1939.

In normal times, Albania exported quantities of wool, dairy products, tobacco, hides, and some cattle. Textiles and other finished products led among imports. Exploited by the Italians, Albania furnished 12,000 auxiliaries to Mussolini's disastrous campaign against Greece in 1940. A large number of these, however, promptly deserted. In the rugged mountain areas of Albania, Italian control was little more than nominal, and the occupation garrisons usually restricted themselves to the few towns, to the through roads, and to the coastal regions.

V. Bulgaria, Hungary, Romania, and Turkey

Since Bulgaria, Romania, and Hungary succumbed to German pressure to become partners of the European Axis, and Turkey remained neutral until the end of World War II, this study will consider these countries but briefly.

Bulgaria, approximately the size of Ohio, had a population of a little more than seven million in 1941. Ethnically close to the Russians, the language of the Bulgarians was Slavonic. With an economy primarily agricultural, the chief Bulgarian exports were fruits and dairy products.

Hungary, not a true Balkan country but adjacent to the Balkan area and continually involved in its problems, had a population of slightly over nine million and was approximately the size of Indiana. The economy of Hungary was agricultural, with meat and cereals the chief exports. Romania, also outside the Balkan area proper, was approximately the size of Oregon, and had a population of fifteen and one-half million, three quarters of whom were engaged in agriculture. With its rich Ploesti fields, Romania was the largest oil producer in the Balkan-Danubian area.

Turkey, as large as Texas and Maine combined, had a population of nineteen and one-half million and an agricultural economy in 1941. In the Balkans proper, Turkey had only a few thousand square miles in eastern Thrace.

CHAPTER 3
TRANSPORTATION AND COMMUNICATIONS

I. General

The rugged terrain of the Balkans proper has been a heavy handicap to the development of an adequate transportation and communication net, and the frequent wars and changes in the political frontiers within the area have made the extension and improvement of facilities even more difficult. Such rail construction as could be compared favorably to that of western Europe in 1941 was restricted to the international lines connecting the capital cities and some lines in the lowland regions in the north.

Although the roads afforded somewhat more complete coverage than the rail lines, there were few hard-surface highways aside from those paralleling the main railroads. The terrain made necessary numerous serpentines and bridges, and detours were often difficult or impossible. On the whole, road repair was very deficient.

Cables connecting the various Balkan capitals were laid before World War I, and some improvements were made during the period preceding the attack in 1941. However, little was done to establish a unified and efficient cable network throughout the Balkan countries.

To remain within the scope of this study, it will be necessary to limit consideration of the transportation and communication net to that of importance to the occupation forces and the irregulars arrayed against them.

II. Main Rail lines

At the time German forces overran the Balkans, Yugoslavia had approximately 6,000 miles and Greece 1,700 miles of railroad lines; both countries used the standard European gauge. The most important lines were those converging on Zagreb from Austria, Italy, and Hungary; the line Zagreb-Belgrade-Nish; and the lines Nish-Sofiya, and Nish-Salonika-Athens. All were vital to the Italian German war effort, since British air and naval activity made supply by sea difficult and the Germans did not have the necessary truck transport facilities. Too, in addition to the occupation forces, those units and installations supporting the German air and naval effort in the eastern Mediterranean had to be supplied by rail, along the line Zagreb-Belgrade-Nish-Salonika-Athens.

III. Principal Highways

The roads of Greece and Yugoslavia were poor, with the exception of a few international highways and limited areas in and about the capitals and major cities. Of the various road nets, the best were those in northwestern Yugoslavia, in the areas taken from the Austro-Hungarian Empire; about Belgrade; through Skoplje to Salonika; in the industrial area about Salonika; and in the Athens-Piraeus industrial and shipping complex.

To the German and Italian occupation forces, the most important road nets were those roughly paralleling the rail lines through northern Yugoslavia, including Belgrade; along the Vardar River to Salonika, thence along the Aegean coast to Athens; a system of roads through the northern half of the Peloponnesus; a series of secondary roads along the Adriatic coast of Yugoslavia; some tortuous roads through the Dinaric Alps; and a few main roads in western Greece. Though some of these roads were paved, the majority were built of crushed stone and unable to support sustained traffic and heavy trucks in any number without constant repair. In many places, lengths of paved road alternated with stretches of crushed stone.

IV. Waterways, Airfields, and Signal Facilities

While the Danube played a significant part in the logistical support of the attack forces, the waterways within Greece and Yugoslavia proper played little part in the later supply of the occupation troops. Perhaps that put to the most extensive use was the Corinth Canal, linking the Gulf of Corinth and the Aegean. By using this canal, the Italians were able to cut the distance from their supply bases along the Adriatic and Ionian Seas to Piraeus and Athens by some 130 miles, avoiding the open sea and British aircraft based in Egypt.

Airfield facilities in Greece and Yugoslavia, though not extensive, were more than adequate for the needs of the Germans and Italians. Stocks of gasoline and other supplies left behind in Greece by the British were put to use, and the slight damage to fighter bases was not enough to prevent their immediate utilization. Perhaps most important strategically were the excellent bases on Crete and in the Athens-Piraeus area.

Signal facilities in the various Balkan countries at the time of the occupation were incapable of supporting heavy traffic. Too, it was a simple matter for the guerrillas to disrupt the few long-distance cables and overhead wires that existed. The mountainous nature of the terrain circumscribed the use of radio, but it was on this and field telephone lines, plus liaison aircraft, that the occupation forces usually had to rely.

PART TWO

THE OCCUPATION OF THE BALKANS AND THE RISE OF THE GUERRILLA MOVEMENT (1941-42)

THE German combat troops, scheduled to leave almost immediately to refit for Operation BARBAROSSA (the assault on the Soviet Union), had little time for prisoners after their quick conquest of Yugoslavia, and captured Greeks were paroled as a gesture of respect for their heroic effort in defense of their country. Thus, shortly after the cessation of hostilities, the Yugoslav and Greek forces were demobilized, their personnel idle, and stunned rather than crushed by their sudden defeat. Many had never seen the enemy, others had recently been on the offensive, as the Greek forces in Albania, and had been forced to stop fighting only when encircled by the Germans or because higher commanders had surrendered.

The German authorities were cognizant of the threat of these unemployed ex-soldiers and other dissident elements uniting to form a resistance movement. Moreover, the commencement of hostilities with the Soviet Union 2 months later made external support of such a movement most probable; aid by the Russians would serve to divert (}German divisions from the Russian theater of war, gain the Kremlin an opening wedge for the communization of the Balkans, and possibly even permanent realization of the age-old Russian desire for access to the Adriatic and Mediterranean. Little was done to forestall the obvious threat of revolt. Perhaps the Germans considered the few divisions they were leaving behind sufficient to secure

Greece and Yugoslavia and keep up an uninterrupted Bow of raw materials to the German war machine. Most certainly German planners were preoccupied with the approaching campaign against the Soviet Union. At any rate, German preparations to contain and destroy large-scale risings were inadequate. Belated German efforts as time passed succeeded only in quelling temporarily the growing surge of resistance in areas where the occupation authorities could mass superior forces. Suppression of the resistance movement became and remained for over 2 years a makeshift affair, with the guerrillas being pursued from one area to another, suffering heavy casualties, but never being destroyed. During this 2-year period, duty in the southeast was regarded as relatively safe by the average landser (soldier); not as pleasant, perhaps, as assignment to occupation duty in France, Belgium, or Holland, but infinitely preferable to service in the Soviet Union or North Africa. For its part, the Armed Forces High Command considered its Balkan theater a bulwark against attack from the south and its possession necessary for the security of the forces in the southern part of the Soviet Union. The Reich's primary interest in the area itself, once these security objectives had been achieved, was as a source of strategic raw materials. Its importance increased when the supply of chrome from Turkey was stopped and the Turks began to drift toward the Allied camp.

The German attitude toward the population was one of mistrust. The majority of the inhabitants were Slavs, and ohne Kultur (lacking culture). However, as in the other occupied countries, the Germans felt they could reach a modus vivendi to achieve their military and political aims; the population could be kept under control by a program of dividing and ruling, well illustrated by the establishment of a Croatian state out of the body of Yugoslavia.

CHAPTER 4

THE OCCUPATION ZONES AND FORCES

I. Division and Dismemberment

To free German troops for employment in Operation
BARBAROSSA and in compliance with commitments to
Mussolini, the occupation of the Balkans was to be primarily a
responsibility of the Italians. German interests in the area, as
defined by Hitler, included only the security of supply routes and
communications to German air bases in Greece and Crete, the
safeguarding of the copper-producing area in northeastern
Serbia, the protection of an open shipping route on the Danube,
and retention of the economic privileges granted Germany by
the former Yugoslav Government.

In addition to Albania, which they had held since 1939, the
Italians assumed control of Greece, with the exception of
German-held areas around Salonika and Athens, the island of
Crete, and a number of the Aegean Islands. Another exception
was western Thrace, which was annexed by the Bulgarians.

In Yugoslavia, the Italians incorporated western Slovenia,
including Ljubljana, into Italy, and annexed Dalmatia and
Montenegro. A small portion of southwestern Serbia was
detached and added to "Greater Albania." The Italians also
dominated the newly proclaimed kingdom of Croatia, which for
purposes of security and antiguerrilla operations was divided
into German and Italian zones of interest by a line along the axis
Visegrad-Sarajevo-Banja Lukanorth to the border of the
German-annexed portion of Slovenia; the Germans were
permitted to send troops into the area east of this line and the
Italian troops could operate west of the line. For their part, the

Germans incorporated into "Greater Germany" that portion of Slovenia that had once been part of the Austrian province of Carinthia, and occupied Serbia and the Banat. The Bulgarians annexed Yugoslav Macedonia and, in early 1942, occupied southeastern Serbia; the Hungarians annexed the Batchka and Baranya and a small portion of eastern Slovenia.

II. The Italians

Three Italian armies and a total of 45 divisions had participated in the campaigns against Greece and Yugoslavia. The armies were the. Second. Ninth and Eleventh, all directly under the Commando Supremo (Supreme General Staff), under which they remained for the period of the occupation. By early August 1941 the army headquarters had been redesignated as area commands and the total number of divisions reduced to 32. The commander of the Italian Second Army became Armed Forces Commander, Slovenia and Dalmatia, with 8 divisions; the commanding general of the Ninth Army became Armed Forces Commander, Albania and Montenegro, with 12 divisions; the Eleventh Army commander became the Armed Forces' Commander, Greece, with 11 divisions. One additional division was stationed in the Dodecanese Islands. A change in this organization was made when the Armed Forces Command, Albania and Montenegro, was divided between the Armed Forces Command, Albania, and the Military Command, Montenegro. The policy of the Italian occupation authorities was wavering and irresolute, and the Italians accomplished little or nothing toward restoring the economy of the areas under their control. Commanders were slow to react to guerrilla forays, and the common soldier hoped for a state of mutual toleration with the population. This reluctance to act firmly, after their poor showing in the 194~41 campaigns, earned the Italians the disdain of the Greeks and Yugoslavs and encouraged depredations. Harsh and arbitrary reprisals, when action was undertaken, further increased the resentment of the population toward the Italians. Individual punishment was often inflicted without trial, and on many occasions entire villages were burned to discourage disorders. From disdain, the attitude of the Greeks and Yugoslavs soon changed to one of hatred.

III. The Germans

The German Twelfth Army, which had driven the length of the Balkan Peninsula and conquered Greece, was assigned to the occupation of the German-held areas in the southeast, with headquarters near Athens, whence it moved on 27 October to Salonika. The commander of Twelfth Army, General-feldmarschall (Field Marshal) Wilhelm List, also became Armed Forces Commander, Southeast, on 9 June 1941, thereafter functioning in a dual role.' As Armed Forces Commander, Southeast, Field Marshal List was the supreme German military authority in the Balkans and was answerable ' directly to Hitler. His responsibilities in this capacity included the preparation and direction of a coordinated defense against attack, the suppression of internal unrest, and the conduct of relations with the Italian and other Axis military authorities in the area. Marshal List was further charged with the security of German supply routes through Balkans and the military administration of the German-occupied areas. These last were three in number: Serbia proper; the Salonika region and the islands of Lemnos, Mytilene, Khios, and Skyros; and southern Greece, including the cities of Athens and Piraeus, and the islands of Crete, Cythera, and Melos. Serbia was placed under the Military Commander, Serbia, with headquarters at Belgrade; the Salonika area under the Military Commander Salonika-Aegean, with headquarters at Salonika; and Athens and Piraeus under the Military Commander, Southern Greece, with headquarters at Athens. Since much of the German air effort in the eastern Mediterranean was directed from Athens, the headquarters of the Military Commander,

A delegation of the Second Proletarian Brigade, Yugoslavia, December 1942.

Southern Greece, was staffed largely by the Air Force. The naval and air force headquarters in the Balkans were placed under control of Marshal List for operational purposes, as were the various liaison officers and military missions with the Italians, Bulgarians, Hungarians, and Croats.

At the time hostilities ended in April, Twelfth f Army had under its control four corps headquarters and a total of twelve divisions, four of them armored. By 22 June, when Operation BARBAROSSA began, three of the corps headquarters, all the armored divisions, and all but 2 mountain and 1 infantry divisions had been redeploycd. This redistribution of forces left Twelfth Army with the XVIII Mountain Corps, with headquarters near Athens, to which were attacked thc 5th and 6th mountain Divisions, on Crete and near Athens, respectively; the 164th Infantry Division, in Salonika and on the Aegean Islands; and the 125th Infantry Regiment (Separate), in Salonika.

The gap created by the departed units was filled partially by the recently created LXV Corps Command, an area, rather than a tactical, headquarters stationed in Belgrade. To this headquarters were attached the 704th, 714th, and 717th Infantry

Divisions, spread over Serbia proper, and the 718th Infantry Division, stationed in the German zone of interest in Croatia, with headquarters at Banja Luka. In contrast to the troops they replaced, more than one-half f of the personnel of these divisions, particularly the platoon leaders and noncommissioned officers, were over age for infantry service. The combat experience of most of the company and higher commanders was limited to World War I, and the divisions lacked their full complement of motor vehicles and logistical services. Training had been interrupted by the assignment to occupation duty to the extent one division had only completed battalion exercises.

German strength in the Balkans remained at approximately this level until mid-September 1941, the only change being in mid-August, when the 6th Mountain Division left. The 713th Infantry Division of the same type as the divisions attached to the LXV Corps Command, moved into the Balkans shortly before the departure of the mountain division.

The military occupation task was made difficult by the presence of various SS and police agencies in the occupied territories. Acting directly under the Reichsfuehrer SS and Chief of German Police Himmler, these agencies were the cause of constant irritation to the military commanders. Ostensibly responsible for security, their activities overlapped those of the military, and local commanders were not permitted to control them or to restrict their activities. Various civilian agencies, such as the German Foreign Office, were also represented in Greece and Yugoslavia, further complicating the task of the military commanders.

The policy of the Germans was stern but consistent, compared to that of the Italians. Serbia presented the Germans with a special problem, however, with the traditional Serb hostility to everything Germanic, the rugged independence of the people, and the former position of predominance the Serbs had held in the Yugoslav state.

IV. The Bulgarians and Hungarians

To maintain order in their new territories, the Bulgarians dispatched their V Corps, composed of three divisions, to Yugoslav Macedonia, and their I Corps to Thrace. A subsequent reassignment of units, with the movement of Bulgarian troops into the German zone in Yugoslavia, brought the I Corps to southeastern Serbia and a provisional "Aegean Corps" to Thrace. Later in the war, the Aegean Corps was relieved by the II Corps. A number of incidents involving the native population in Macedonia caused the Bulgarians to turn from a benevolent to a harsh policy of pacification. In Greece, where they felt they were recovering territory lost to the Greeks in the Second Balkan War of 1913, the policy of the Bulgarians was arbitrary and severe from the outset of the occupation.

The Hungarians occupied several small areas of Yugoslavia to the west and south of Hungary, and immediately incorporated them into their national state. Inhabited by large Hungarian minorities, these territories had formed part of the Austro-Hungarian Empire until 1918, hence the Hungarian attitude toward the population was far more lenient than that of the other occupation forces in their respective zones.

V. The Puppet Governments

Puppet regimes were installed to lighten the administrative burden of the occupied areas and exploit the differences between the various Greek and Yugoslav national and political factions. Native police, security forces, and national armies were also organized to reduce the number of occupation troops required to keep order and protect the various new governments.

The collaborationist regime in Greece was organized under the premiership of General Tsolakoglou, who had surrendered the Army of Epirus to the Germans on 20 April 1941. Although this government formed police and security units and actively assisted the German and Italian occupiers, it did not organize armed forces on a national scale.

In Croatia a kingdom was organized under the nominal rule of the absentee Italian Duke of Spoleto, with actual authority vested in Ante Pavelitch, the Poglavnik (Prime Minister), who began his administration with a ruthless persecution of the Serbian minority within the borders of the new Croatian state.

Pavelitch, living in exile under Italian sponsorship, had been indirectly involved in the assassination of King Alexander of Yugoslavia at Marseilles in 1934. Arriving in Croatia in the wake of the Germans in 1941 with fewer than a hundred of his Ustascha, a politico-military group, similar to the Italian Blackshirts, Pavelitch quickly organized a political army of 15 battalions, and a Ustascha Guard of 1 infantry regiment and a cavalry squadron. Under the aegis of the Italian authorities, he also began the conscription of a national military force, which did not progress beyond eight mountain and light infantry brigades and a railroad security brigade until late in the war, when these brigades were joined with the expanded Ustascha forces to form divisions. Croatian-German "Legion" units, such as the 369th, 373d, and 392d Infantry Divisions; two SS divisions, the 13th and 23d Mountain; and additional mountain brigades and separate battalions were recruited in Croatia by the Germans draining off much of the manpower that might have gone to the Croatian forces. More potential Croatian troops were siphoned off in labor drafts or by the police, or fled to join one or another of the guerrilla groups.

A Petain-like figure was found in Serbia in the person of General Neditch, a former chief of staff of the Royal Yugoslav Army. Within Serbin, in addition to the civil police, several militarized security forces were formed to keep order and lighten the German occupation task. The first of these was the Border Guard, 5,600 strong, including a German cadre of 600; the primary mission of this force was to control traffic across the Serbian frontier. In addition, to support the city and rural police should the need arise, the State Guard was organized, comprising five battalions with an authorized total strength of 3,560 men.

The Serbian Volunteer Battalions, later amalgamated into the Serbian Volunteer Corps, most closely approximated a national military force. Four and later five in number, these battalions, under the command of General Ljotitch, were scattered about the German-occupied area of Serbia. Their approximate total strength was 2,000.

Another force formed in 1941 within Serbia but not responsible to the Neditch Government was the Russian Guard Corps, under command of General Steifon. It had three regiments and a total strength of 4,000. Incorporated into the Wehrmacht, the corps was composed largely of anti-Soviet émigrés who had served in the armies of the Czar; many of the personnel were incapable of extended field service, and the Germans generally restricted them to such security duties as the protection of the vital Belgrade-Nish railroad line.

CHAPTER 5

THE EARLY MOVEMENT AND AXIS COUNTERMEASURES

THE political allegiances of the resistance movement had little influence on the military operations conducted by the occupying powers Rather, everyone fighting against the occupation forces was considered a threat to their hold on the Balkans. True, the methods used and the ultimate objectives differed from one group to the other. However. as far as the Italians, Germans, and Bulgarians were concerned, all in arms against them were enemies, whether they w ore the royal crest of a sovereign in exile, the hammer and sickle, or no insignia whatever.

I. Yugoslavia

Armed opposition on a significant scale received its start in Yugoslavia. However, any consideration of this movement would be incomplete without distinguishing between the Pan-Serb, monarchical group of the former Col. Draja Mihailovitch and the communist-led effort of Josip Broz, or Tito. It was the former that first came to the attention of the Allied world, at the time German domination of the Continent was almost complete and Soviet forces were retreating from western Russia.

Mihailovitch called his irregulars "Chetniks," from the title of the Serb nationalist organization that had resisted the Turks, fought well in World War I, and since existed as a reserve force to be called up when needed. Costa Pecanatch, the aging World War I leader, went over to the Neditch government at the outset of the occupation, leaving Mihailovitch with those remnants willing to resist the occupation forces and collaborationists. The

Serbian Commander Tito inspecting his troops

Mihailovitch movement quickly gained momentum during the early summer of 1941, and liaison was established with the government-in-exile of King, Peter. A short time later Mihailovitch was first named commander of the resistance forces within Yugoslavia, and then minister of defense of the royal government-in-exile.

Chetnik policy called for the organization of strong underground forces in Serbia for the day when they might rise in conjunction with Allied landings on the Balkan Peninsula. Mihailovitch, himself, had been appalled by the execution of some 35,000 Serb hostages for Chetnik activities in World War I, and was determined to avoid repetition of any such reprisals for a premature rising of the forces under his command. Thus, Chetnik operations were generally restricted to small-scale actions and sabotage.

It was the communist irregulars who adopted the name of Partisan and made it synonymous with guerrilla. Under Tito, born Josip Broz in Croatia, converted to communism while a prisoner of war of the Russians at the time of the Red Revolution, and Secretary General of the Communist Party of

Yugoslavia since 1937, the Partisan movement received its start in Belgrade immediately after the surrender to the Germans. In August 1941 Tito moved his headquarters into the field and took over command of the growing Partisan forces. The antiroyalist policy of the Partisans and anti-Communist attitude of the Chetniks soon led to a fratricidal conflict between the two, a cleavage the Germans were quick to turn to their own advantage. Whereas the Chetniks comprised mostly local units to be called up as needed, the Partisans had a great number of large and active mobile units capable of moving about the country and not tied down to any particular locality. As a consequence, the Partisans were not as hesitant as the Chetniks to engage in operations for which the occupying forces would exact severe reprisals, a development that incurred further the enmity of the Chetniks. A conflict within a conflict soon developed, with one Yugoslav force attacking the other while that force was already engaged against occupation troops.

In some cases the Partisans were given credit for Chetnik attacks against the occupation forces and their auxiliaries; on the other hand, the Chetniks were credited with successful Partisan forays. To complicate matters further, there were also guerrilla bands operating under no other authority than their own. Thus, German references to Partisans did not necessarily mean the forces of Tito, but rather the Yugoslav resistance forces in general, regardless of political sympathies. As well as the European Axis came to know them, it could not always distinguish one group from the other, and came to use the word Partisan in its broadest sense.

The most important guerrilla operation in 1941 took place against the Italians in Montenegro. Ruggedly independent, the Montenegrins on 13 July swarmed down in well-coordinated attacks on the Italian garrisons scattered throughout their mountain state. Taken by surprise, the occupation forces were destroyed or thrown back on their major garrison towns and communications centers. Returning with strong ground, naval, and air forces, the Italians required almost a year to put down the rising, and managed to accomplish it only by enlisting the aid of the Chetniks. Stipulations in the agreement with local Chetnik leaders required the Italians to restrict themselves to the garrison towns and main communication and transportation lines. In turn, the Chetniks maintained control over the countryside and kept it free of Partisans, drawing on Italian stocks for arms and ammunition.

This general rising cost the Montenegrins dearly -15,000 dead and wounded and an additional 10,000 of the sparse mountain population shipped off to forced labor. The arrangement with the Chetniks also set the pattern for the Italian occupation-troops seldom moved out of the garrison towns, and then only along the main roads and in strength, accompanied by armored vehicles and often under air cover.

One other major countermeasure by the Italian occupation forces against the irregulars was undertaken in July of 1942 when General di Corpo D'Armata (Lieutenant General) Mario Robotti launched a drive against the Partisans in Slovenia. Committing 7 army divisions Blackshirt battalions, and Slovene auxiliaries, General Robotti managed to surround the enemy. Several thousand casualties were inflicted on the Partisans, and the survivors were routed. The Partisan movement in Slovenia in this operation suffered a setback from which it did not recover for months.

Guerrilla activities against the Germans in Yugoslavia commenced shortly after the cessation of formal hostilities. However, in the beginning, open resistance to the German forces was on a smaller scale than in the Italian-occupied areas, and the guerrillas conducted themselves more cautiously. With the departure, by late June 1941, of the bulk of the combat troops for Operation BARBAROSSA, the WB Southeast reported an increasing number of sabotage incidents. Road and railroad

Yugoslavian partisans from Montenegro

bridges were blown; telephone and telegraph lines were cut; trains derailed; German military vehicles, traveling either alone or in convoy, fired on or destroyed; and isolated detachments guarding industrial and military installations attacked. During July and August there were also daily attacks on Serbian police posts to obtain weapons and on villages to obtain food. Standing crops were burned, banks robbed, and a general state of uncertainty and unrest created.

A number of small-scale operations by the 704th, 714th, 717th, and 718th Infantry Divisions, dispersed over Serbia and the German zone of interest in Croatia, resulted in a large number of casualties and arrests, but accomplished little in effectively curbing the guerrilla movement. Nor did the shooting of hostages or burning of homes of suspects and whole communities suspected of sheltering the guerrillas achieve the desired results. By 5 September the WB Southeast realized that the situation could not be mastered with the forces at hand and ordered the 125th Infantry Regiment (Separate) from the Salonika area to Belgrade.

It was now obvious that a strong, well-organized, and adequately armed revolt was underway in northwestern Serbia, and that the remainder of German-occupied Serbia w as seriously threatened The spreading disorders were also affecting the supply of vital raw materials, to the extent that in the third quarter of 1041 the destruction of installations in the Bor mining area (northeast of Nish) caused a production loss of nearly a month's requirement of copper for the German war industries. In view of this increasingly critical situation, the Armed Forces Commander, Southeast, was forced to concentrate his meager and scattered forces for the defense of those cities, industrial installations, and transportation lines considered most vital to the German occupation. Further, he requested that the Armed Forces High Command have established a unified command for operations in Serbia under the commander of the XVIII Mountain Corps, General der Gebirgstruppen (Lieutenant General) Franz Boehme. Marshal List further recommended that General Boehme be assigned a combat infantry division and armored support, to supplement the divisions immediately available.

In response to this request, on 16 September Hitler issued a directive that charged Marshal List with suppressing the revolt in the southeast. To accomplish this, he was to place General Boehme in complete charge of operations in Serbia and the adjacent areas in which the irregulars had established themselves. General Boehme was to have command of all troops in the area and of any others that might be moved in; all military and civil authorities were required to carry out General Boehme's orders insofar as they pertained to his mission. The Army High Command was ordered to reinforce the troops in Serbia by one infantry division, armored trains, captured tanks, and further security forces; other captured tanks and security troops were to be sent to Croatia. Another infantry division from the Eastern Front was to be transferred to Serbia when it became available. The Hungarian, Romanian, and Bulgarian forces could be called upon to assist in the operations with the permission of the Armed Forces High Command; the use of Croatian forces available in the German zone of interest adjacent to the Serbian border was approved. The Italians had been informed of the contemplated operations and had been asked to cooperate. In addition, the German Foreign Office was simultaneously to carry out a political offensive in cooperation with the puppet and allied governments against communist centers in the Balkan countries. Implementation of this directive followed swiftly. Three days later General Boehme moved with his headquarters from Salonika and assumed command in Belgrade, and less than one week following this the 342d Infantry Division arrived from Germany.

A series of vigorous offensive operations begun by General Boehme succeeded in quelling the open revolt in western Serbia and indicting over 2,000 casualties on the guerrillas by mid-December. For these operations, General Boehme committed the 342d Infantry Division; the 125th Infantry Regiment (Separate); the 113th Infantry Division, which had arrived from Germany late in November; and the 704th and 714th Infantry Divisions. The guerrillas, however, were not annihilated; large numbers fled into the more mountainous regions and into Croatia, where a new center of open revolt was soon formed.

As of 25 October, Marshal List had been forced to relinquish his duties because of illness, and General der Pioniere (Lieutenant General) Walter Kuntze was appointed acting Armed Forces Commander, Southeast. In early December orders were to move the XVIII Mountain Corps, the only tactical corps headquarters in the Southeast, to Germany. General Boehme's command functions in Serbia were transferred to the commander of the LXV Corps Command, General der Artillery (Lieutenant

General) Paul Bader.

This loss was shortly followed by another, when the serious situation in Russia made necessary the transfer of both the 342d and 113th Infantry Divisions by the end of January 1942. This reduction of forces prompted the German Armed Forces High Command to request the Bulgarians to move troops into southeastern Serbia. The Bulgarians assented and immediately shifted their I Corps from Thrace. Since it was occupying that part of Serbia allocated as an occupation zone of the Germans, the Bulgarian I Corps later came under the operational control of the German Military Commander, Serbia.

The Bulgarian command in Yugoslavia had a pacification problem similar to that of the Germans. Consequently, the Bulgarians undertook a number of antiguerrilla operations on their own initiative, informing the Germans through liaison officers of the results of their efforts. In general, these were so savage as to quell the growth of any resistance movement of significance until late the following year.

Croatia, with its own armed forces, had little success in putting down the spreading Partisan movement within its borders during late 1941. By the end of the year, additional German troops had crossed the borders of the new state into the German zone of interest in order to cooperate with the Ustascha and Croat national forces in hunting flown the Partisans in the southeastern part of the country. Resistance to the Croat troops w as intensified by their persecution of the Serbian minority. The Italian Second Army was of little help in restoring order; Italian units in the area assisting the Germans and Croats showed more interest in occupying important transportation and communication centers than in clearing Croatia of the guerrillas.

With Serbia quiet and the guerrilla forces active in their zone of interest in Croatia, the Germans planned a large-scale operation Italian blocking forces to be brought up to the Italian side of the demarcation line. Planned for mid-January 1942, the operation would have the advantage of cold weather, inconvenient for the Germans but disastrous for the guerrillas, who lacked proper clothing and equipment for operations in the snow. Also, the 342d Infantry Division would be available, just prior to its departure for Russia.

Well planned and typical of antiguerrilla measures of the period, the operation was conducted from 15 to 26 January, with the 342d and 718th Infantry Divisions, as well as Croatian national forces, participating. The guerrillas were estimated at 4,000, concentrated about Sarajevo and Visegrad and the area to the north. Meeting strong resistance, the Germans suffered a total of 25 dead, 131 wounded, and almost 300 cases of frostbite, against 521 guerrilla dead and 1,331 captured. Booty included 855 rifles, 22 machine guns, 4 field pieces, 600 head of livestock, and 33 draft animals. A tactical success, the operation failed to achieve its purpose when the Italian forces against which the guerrillas were to be driven did not arrive in time to prevent the escape of large numbers of the guerrillas into the Italian zone of interest in Croatia.

Reports from German commanders who had participated indicated that the Croatian troops could perform satisfactorily only when integrated with German units, and that the Croat officers and noncommissioned officers lacked training and tactical ability. The escape of entire guerrilla units also made obvious the need for a combined command, with authority over all German, Italian, Croatian, and other forces participating. On one occasion, during the operation, Italian airmen bombed a German-held village, whereupon the Germans requested Italian air support be withdrawn. Another mistake was the assignment of Ustascha troops to areas populated mainly by Serbs. Finally, the understrength German divisions (two regiments of infantry rather than the normal three) in the "700 series" in the southeast lacked personnel and staying power for sustained operations against strong guerrilla forces. Sharp fighting at Valjevo in

February caused the Germans almost 500 casualties, as against over 3,500 guerrillas killed in action or shot in reprisal. Lacking troops, it was obvious that General Kuntze would require the assistance of the Italians and Croatians if his meager forces in Croatia were to quell the disorders in the German zone of interest.

A trip to Hitler's headquarters and to Italy was instrumental in securing approval for a combined German-Italian-Croatian operntion to clear east Bosnia. General Bader, now commanding all German forces and the administrative area in Serbia, was named task force commander, under operational control of the Italian Second Army for the period of the operation. His force was to consist of three Italian divisions, the German 718th Infantry Division, German units from Serbia, and Croatian national troops. Extending from 20 April to 3 May, the operation was considered a success from the German standpoint, with 168 enemy dead, 1,309 prisoners taken, and stocks of weapons, ammunition, and equipment captured. However, large numbers of guerrillas managed to escape through the Italian Units assigned to block their flight and to snake their way into the Italian zone of interest in Croatia. Task Force Bader was disbanded upon conclusion of the operation, and its commander returned to Serbia.

Another operation, to clear west Bosnia, was scheduled for June. The task force commander, Generalmajor (Brigadier General) Friedrich Stahl, commanding the 714th Infantry Division, organized his combat elements around three German infantry battalions with artillery support and two Croatian mountain brigades. No exact figures on casualties were given, but the cost to the guerrillas w as high and the undertaking was regarded as a success by the Germans. The lack of experience and tactical ability on the part of the Croat troops were made glaringly obvious during the operation, when the two mountain brigades broke in disorder and German troops had to strengthen them.

Following the conclusion of the operation in west Bosnia, the divisions in Serbia and Croatia were redisposed. While the 718th Infantry Division remained in east Bosnia, the 714th Infantry Division was assigned to west Bosnia. The 704th Infantry Division remained in eastern Serbia, and the 717th Infantry Division was shifted from southwestern to northwestern Serbia. In turn, the 7th SS Mountain Division (Prinz Eugen), recently formed with ethnic German personnel from Yugoslavia and Romania, was assigned the area evacuated by the 717th Division.

The modest successes of the recent German operations in Bosnia were offset at this time by the withdrawal of the Italian garrisons disposed along the Italian side of the German-Italian demarcation line. The military vacuum created in the area by this withdrawal was immediately used to advantage by the guerrillas, who now had no occupation force with which to contend. The withdrawal was in accordance with an earlier Italian decision to reduce their Second Army garrisons and relinquish control of the interior of Croatia to Croat national forces. To this end, the Italian command had divided its zone of interest into three areas, numbered from one to three, and roughly parallel to the demarcation line and the coast. The third zone, adjoining the German area of interest, was abandoned first, despite German protests that guerrilla activities would increase.

A German recapitulation of casualties sustained by the Yugoslav guerrillas from the beginning of the occupation to July 1942 estimated the total at 45,000 dead with thousands more sent off to forced labor in Germany and occupied areas as far away as Norway, or detained in internment camps. In addition to the arrestees shipped out of the country the Germans added a large number of former Yugoslav officials as a security measure, whether or not any involvement with the guerrillas could be proved against them.

The German forces in Croatia and Serbia carried out a series of small-scale operations throughout the remainder of the year without achieving any marked success in eliminating the guerrilla movement. There was an increase in troop strength with the the Reserve Division arrived in Croatia by December. In October, a new headquarters, that of Commander of German Troops in Croatia, under Generalleutnant (Major General) Rudolf Lueters, was created; however, this headquarters did not become operational until shortly after the end of the year.

II. Greece

The Greek resistance movement, like the Yugoslavia, was divided along political lines between the groups adhering to the royal government-in-exile and those led or strongly influence by communists. In Greece the former were led by a Colonel Zervas, a retired officer of the Greek Regular Army; the latter, by a Colonel Sarafis, dismissed from the Regular Army for political activities in January 1935. The Zervas organization, known as EDES (Greek Democratic National League), was restricted to the mountains of Epirus in northwestern Greece; ELAS (Greek People's Liberation Army) operated in the rest of the country. While EDES maintained contact with the Greek Government-in-Exile, ELAS functioned under EAM (National Liberation Front), a coalition of left-wing parties with a hard core of Communists. Another guerrilla group, socialist in nature and associated loosely with ELAS, was known as EKKA (National and Social Liberation); it was led by a Colonel Psarros and operated in central Greece.

Unlike those in Yugoslavia, the Greek guerrillas undertook no operations of importance in 1941. For their part, the Germans were more concerned with fortifying Crete, pursuing their air effort in the eastern Mediterranean from Greek bases, and getting all combat forces that could be spared to the more active theaters of war. In late October the 5th Mountain Division was moved from Crete to Germany, being replaced by the weak 164th and 713th Infantry Divisions from the Athens and Salonika areas; these two divisions were then disbanded to form Fortress Division, Crete. The garrison on Crete received further reinforcement in the 125th Infantry Regiment (Separate), moved down from Serbia, where it had proved itself in heavy antiguerrilla fighting. An example of guerrilla operations in Greece in 1942 is provided by an attack of the Zervas group on an Italian supply column on the Yannina-Arta road during the summer. This completely successful attack, in which approximately one hundred guerrillas annihilated a heavily armed force of sixty men and captured or destroyed a large stock of ammunition and gasoline, was carefully prepared and vigorously executed. The attack was made under difficult conditions, in that Italian forces were in control of the area and had held it for more than a year allowing them ample opportunity to recruit informants, know the population well enough to detect new arrivals, and reconnoiter the terrain. In addition, the Italians were amply supplied with signal equipment, automatic weapons, and armored vehicles, while the guerrillas had not yet captured any appreciable number of arms or received any substantial supplies from the Allies. Except for a few machine-guns and mines, the only weapons of the attackers were rifles and dynamite.

After several weeks of studying Italian dispositions and movements in the area, the guerrillas decided that an attack on the heavily loaded supply column regularly carrying gasoline and ammunition from Yannina to Arta offered the best prospect of success. Accordingly, the guerrilla command chose a defile along the road, out of sight of any inhabited locality, where rocky ledges on either side offered cover to ambushes. Mines could be used to stop the lead vehicle, while a bridge to the rear could be blown to block the column's withdrawal.

On the day of the attack, the guerrillas occupied their hiding places before daylight and waited throughout the day. Telephone and telegraph poles along the road had been cut almost through, so that they could be pulled down with little effort just prior to the action, effectively eliminating any wire communication between the garrisons at Arta and Yannina. Large boulders had been rolled into position on the higher ledges and so placed as to require only a slight pressure to send them tumbling down onto the column halted below. The few machine-guns were sited to allow enfilading fire the length of the column, while the gun crews had the protection of the stone ledges against flat trajectory fire from below.

The Italian column appeared at 1600 and was halted exactly as planned when the lead vehicle, a tank, was disabled by mines. The last vehicle, also a tank, was trapped when the bridge behind it was blown a minute later. The column commander became a casualty almost immediately, and the alarmed troops added to the confusion by firing their automatic weapons blindly at the ledges above. The only organized resistance, which caused a number of casualties to the attackers, came from the crew of the tank at the tail of the column. this vehicle was soon put out of action by a dynamite charge. After raking the column repeatedly with heavy fire, the guerrillas swarmed down onto the roadway and slaughtered the few dazed Italians remaining; no prisoners were taken. The supplies carried by the column were quickly loaded onto pack animals brought up for the purpose, while roadblocks secured the attackers against surprise by relief columns from Arta or Yannina.

As planned by the attackers, approaching darkness made pursuit impossible. A motorcycle platoon sent out from Arta to investigate the disruption of wire communications was stopped by fire at the roadblock south of the site of the ambush and no further relief was attempted until morning, by which time the guerrillas were safely away.

Although the supply column had been heavily armed, the

Italian commander had made a mistake that was often to cost the occupation forces heavily-he had followed a fixed pattern in moving critical supplies along the same route at regular intervals, making it possible for the guerrillas to determine the schedule, the strength of the escort, and observe the practice of having the only armored vehicles at the head and tail. Such successful attacks emboldened the resistance forces and inclined recruits to join their ranks or to assist them in various other ways, such as reporting troop movements. During July and August, Fortress Division Crete was sent to Africa, and redesignated the 164th Light Africa Division. In its place, the 22d Airborne Division was moved in from Russia and assigned to garrison the island fortress.

On 8 August, the acting Armed Forces Commander, Southeast, General Kuntze, vas relieved by Generaloberst (General) Alexander Loehr. General Loehr, a Luftwaffe officer, had been in command of the Fourth Air Force in Russia before receiving his new appointment as commander in the Balkans; he had also commanded the task force which captured Crete in May 1941.

Guerrilla operations in Greece were not restricted to ambushes. Sabotage, particularly along the vital Athens-Salonika rail line, also played an important part in hampering the supply of the occupation forces and tying down units to perform security duties. The most significant sabotage operation was executed on 25 November, when a small guerrilla force overpowered Italian guards and blew up the Gorgopotamos Bridge. some hundred miles north of Athens. This successful operation not only halted the flow of supplies until repairs could be effected, but led to severe criticism of the Italians by the Germans and made it necessary for the Germans to take over the security of a long stretch of this rail line in Italian-occupied territory, a strain on the already insufficient German forces and a rebuff to Italian pride.

Additional troops were moved into the Greek area in December, as a result of the Allied landings in Africa one month earlier. The threat presented by United States and British forces to his position in the eastern Mediterranean prompted Hitler shortly afterward to direct immediate reinforcements to be sent to General Loehr. Accordingly, the 11th Luftwaffe Field Division moved into Attica, north of Athens. Though the original purpose in sending the 11th Field Division to Greece had been to replace the 22d Airborne Division, the worsening strategic situation required the retention of both divisions. As a result, the 11th Field Division took over responsibility for a considerable area of Attica and the 22d Division remained as a mobile and potent striking force to counter possible Allied landings on Crete. By the end of 1942, the Greek resistance forces were still in the process of formation, having no centralized command. While Chetniks and Partisans in Yugoslavia had already established higher headquarters to direct operations, and were receiving quantities of supplies from the British forces in the Middle East, the Greek resistance units were recruiting personnel and leaders of such stature as to command the respect and win the support of the population.

CHAPTER 6

ORGANIZATION OF GUERRILLA UNITS

I. Unit and Command Structure

Most of the early guerrilla groups in Greece and Yugoslavia were Organized on a regional basis, taking as a unit designation the name of their leader or of the area, or of such geographical features as forests or mountains. In time, such leaders as Zervas, Sarafis, Mihailovitch, and Tito arose, and the various groups divided along political lines. As they expanded, it became necessary to form military units.

In Greece the units were organized and designated along the lines of the regular forces of the prewar period, with companies, battalions, regiments, and divisions. In Yugoslavia the odreds (groups) became brigades, above which higher headquarters were formed to exercise control. Since the forces in both countries were still on a militia basis, the Greek and Yugoslav commands also found it expedient to form mobile units, which would not be tied down to any particular region and could be sent where needed. Captured arms, as well as materiel supplied by the Allies, soon permitted the mobile units to take on the semblance of regular troops, with automatic weapons, mortars, antitank guns, and even light field pieces to support their riflemen.

The military designations of brigade, division, and corps, however, were no indication of actual strength. For example, ELAS at one time had 10 organizations carried as divisions, but a total strength of only 30,000; the brigades of Tito's Partisans frequently had only a few hundred men.

In the Partisan force, the chain of command went through

brigade, division, corps, and area headquarters, and then to Tito's staff, which had a status comparable to that of an army. Tito himself professed to be the commander of the armed forces of the independent state of Yugoslavia.

The Chetnik organization was based on a "brigade" of two combat companies and a replacement company. Three to eight brigades formed a corps, subordinate to an area headquarters responsible to Mihailovitch, at approximately army level. As Yugoslav Minister of Defense, Mihailovitch was a member of the Yugoslav Government-in-Exile and responsible to the Prime Minister and King Peter.

Authority in ELAS extended from company through division, also an area command, to ELAS headquarters, which was comparable to a corps with ten divisions. When ELAS reached this point in its development, intermediate headquarters so-called groups of divisions were formed, and ELAS headquarters assumed army status. The Central Committee of EAM, in turn, exercised executive direction over ELAS headquarters.

The EDES group by the end of 1942 comprised only a battalion and a number of smaller units. EDES headquarters itself was subordinated to the British Middle East forces and the Greek Government-in-Exile. A number of attempts were made, chiefly by the Allies, to combine the efforts of the rival Greek and Yugoslav guerrilla armies. Although a combined Greek headquarters was actually formed and functioned for a time, opposing political aspirations soon brought ELAS and EDES into open conflict with one another again. In Yugoslavia, attempts to unite the Chetnik and Partisan movements progressed no farther than a brief conference Between Tito and Mihailovitch at the town of Uzice in 1941.

II. Communications and Supply

Closely connected with the command structure was the problem of signal communications. For forces like the Greek and

Yugoslav guerrilla units, fighting for survival in enemy-occupied territory, adequate communications were vital. Since the occupation troops were in possession of the telegraph stations, telephone exchanges, and such radio transmitters as existed in the two countries, the resistance leaders were forced to rely on two other media of communication, courier and radio. Where the former sufficed for short-range work and the delivery of funds and some messages, it could hardly be used for frequent communication between widely separated units and with Allied headquarters across the Mediterranean and Adriatic Seas. Therefore, despite difficulties in transmission and reception in mountain areas, the various guerrilla leaders came to make increasing use of the air waves. For security reasons they did much of their own cryptographic work, until Allied liaison teams with trained personnel were assigned to them. However, a considerable volume of transmission between units was still carried on in the clear by poorly trained native operators, and the Germans were not slow to seize upon the opportunity to gain information. For example, within 60 days of setting up its monitoring devices, one German intercept platoon was able to compile the complete order of battle of the Chetnik forces, including identification and strength of major units, names of commanders, and locations of headquarters.

As the irregular forces grew in size, the problem of feeding increased apace. Since Greece was a food-importing country even in peacetime, the situation in that country was particularly acute. In Yugoslavia, which normally had a surplus and exported large quantities of grain, the matter of rations was critical only in certain unproductive areas such as the mountains of Bosnia, or in localities where the occupation forces had seized and removed large stocks of food.

A distinction must also be made between the static and mobile guerrilla units; the former lived as peasants or tradesmen when not engaged in operations and could support themselves, while the latter had to remain in hiding and could seldom provide their own sustenance. The mobile units then began the practice of requisitioning food in rural areas, since sufficient rations could not be acquired from captured stores and the Allied airlift brought in mostly weapons, ammunition, explosives, and other combat equipment. In the early period, villages in each group's area were assessed specified quantities of produce, which were usually picked up at night. On occasion the guerrilla groups clashed with one another when one group encroached upon another's territory to procure food supplies; sometimes the peasants themselves resisted requisitioning.

As old Greek and Yugoslav uniforms wore out, the guerrillas turned to the occupation forces and civilian population for replacements. In time, a large number of the irregulars were clad in pieces of German and Italian uniforms or cast-oaf civilian clothing. Later, when supplies in bulk were received from the Allies, many of the guerrillas were issued one-piece khaki uniforms, on which they wore as insignia the royal arms or the hammer and sickle, with or without designation of rank.

The first Allied liaison officers had been assigned to Yugoslav resistance units by late 1941 and to the Greeks in the course of 1942. As these units cleared larger areas of occupation forces, it soon became possible to bring in increasing quantities of materiel and supplies by air. Requests for specific equipment and stores were made by guerrilla commanders to the liaison officers, and transmitted to the British forces in the Middle East and later to Allied Forces Headquarters in Italy. Supplies were also moved in by submarine and small boat along unguarded stretches of the coast.

III. Training and Tactics

The training of the guerrillas centered about the use of rifles and light automatic weapons, the laying of mines, and the preparation of demolitions. Former members of the Greek and

Yugoslav forces usually received about 2 weeks of instruction. However, as casualties mounted and the guerrilla forces gained in size, many youths with no previous military experience were enlisted and given from 4 to 6 weeks of basic training. The intensity of training depended to a large extent on the ability of the local commander and the need for the troops in operations. Shortage of ammunition often required that firing be held to the minimum during training. In addition to work with his individual weapon, the guerrilla also learned to lay mines, plant demolition charges, and execute ambushes. Night marches and stealth in movement were stressed, and the guerrillas were instructed never to abandon their dead or wounded to the enemy. Security was also given proper emphasis, and in communist units political indoctrination filled a large part of the training schedule.

Discipline was strict, with lesser crimes punished by public admonition, loss of rank, relief from command, or prohibition from bearing arms for a specified period of time. Serious offenses, such as treason and cowardice, were punished by death, the execution being carried out by the offender's immediate superior. Attacks were carefully planned, taking full advantage of any weakness or carelessness of the occupation forces. The tactic most commonly practiced was the ambush, so timed that the attackers would be well away before the arrival of any relief: mobile units would retire to prearranged hiding places, and the militiamen would return to their homes and regular occupations.

Laying mines and planting demolitions by night were other operations favored by the guerrillas. Designed to cripple transportation and communications and cause casualties, these tactics also tied down engineer personnel who might have been put to other tasks or made available for assignment to active fronts.

Sniping at individual soldiers and small parties also was common practice, as was the cutting of telephone lines and the mining of poles that had to be climbed before repairs could be effected. In the latter case, the lineman working in his exposed position on the pole could be shot if the mine were not effective.

Finally, there was an almost universal disregard on the part of the guerrilla forces, particularly the communists, for the accepted customs and usages of war. Hospitals, ambulance convoys, and hospital trains, lacking any protection but the small arms carried by officers and enlisted orderlies, were easy targets to attack and particularly inviting, since the guerrillas suffered from a chronic shortage of medical supplies. The sick and wounded would be slain in their beds, the medical stores looted, and on occasion captured doctors and other medical personnel would be carried along and forced to care for sick and wounded guerrillas. The shortage of clothing and the necessity of obtaining uniforms for purposes of disguise soon made the stripping of all corpses a common practice, and extremists among the irregulars would mutilate both living and dead in exacting personal vengeance. These acts of terrorism incurred savage retaliation by the Germans and their allies, and increased the fury of the struggle.

PART THREE

THE GUERRILLA MOVEMENT IN GREECE, YUGOSLAVIA, AND ALBANIA (1943-44)

THE German prospect of victory had begun to fade by the beginning of 1943. Stalingrad would cost the Germans 22 divisions and 300,000 men of the Sixth Army by February, and Axis forces in North Africa would be forced to surrender to the Allies in May. The growing losses on all fronts could no longer be replaced in full, and Fortress Europe was threatened by invasion from the south. In their zones of Greece and Yugoslavia, the Germans were plagued by attacks on small outposts and transportation lines, sapping their strength, tying down units and equipment urgently needed in the active theaters of war, and hampering the organization of an effective defense against Allied landings. The growing strength of the resistance forces was felt even more by Germany's Croatian and Italian allies, who had abandoned extensive areas of the countryside to the irregulars and restricted themselves to securing the larger centers of population and the main roads and rail lines. This withdrawal even permitted the organization by the Partisans of a provisional government in Bosnia.

The significance of these developments was not lost on the German Armed Forces High Command, which had issued a directive, over Hitler's signature on 28 December 1942, raising the status of the Armed Forces Commander, Southeast, to that of Commander-in-Chief, Southeast and his force to that of an army group. General Loehr was enjoined, as Marshal List had been more than a year earlier, to establish adequate defenses against Allied landings, and to destroy all guerrilla groups in his rear, since they threatened the accomplishment of his mission.

CHAPTER 7

OPERATIONS (JANUARY-AUGUST 1943)

I. Yugoslavia

It w as evident that neither the Pavelitch government nor the Italian forces in Croatia could cope with the widespread activities of the Partisans. Accordingly, it devolved upon General Lueters, Commander of German Troops in Croatia, to take appropriate measures.

General Lueter's first large-scale action was Operation WEISS. This was to be executed in conjunction with Italian forces, with the mission of annihilating strong Partisan units in the mountainous region west and northwest of Sarajevo. The operation was to be completed in three phases, with Italian troops holding zone two on the Italian side of the demarcation line and allowing the Germans to move into zone three, evacuated some time previously and heavily infiltrated by the guerrillas.

The German force committed to WEISS included the 7th SS Mountain and 717th Infantry Divisions, the recently arrived 369th Infantry Division, and a regiment of the 187th Infantry Division. The Italian force was the V Corps of the Italian Second' Army. In sharp fighting in the first phase of WEISS, the Germans and their allies inflicted more than 8,500 casualties on the Partisans, taking 2,010 prisoners. The German losses totaled 335 dead and 101 missing with Croatian losses in proportion; Italian casualties were markedly lighter, since the Italian units lacked aggressiveness and the proper balance in heavy weapons to engage in sustained fire fights. WEISS I was concluded on 18 February, and the divisions immediately regrouped for the second phase, to be completed by mid-March.

Heavy fighting marked the opening of WEISS II. Additional troops of the VI Corps in Montenegro arrived to bolster the Italian force, but substantial numbers of Partisans managed to break through the Italian line and escape south and southeast into the wilder mountain regions of Herzegovina, Montenegro, and eastern Bosnia. Dispersing into almost inaccessible areas, the Partisan command group and numerous individuals managed to elude their pursuers. WEISS III, the Italian part of the operation, was completely unsuccessful.

WEISS was satisfactory from the German point of view in that the important bauxite-producing area of Yugoslavia was cleared of Partisans and heavy casualties were inflicted among them in the process populated mountain areas offering little sustenance and few recruits to replace the battle losses.

The Chetniks became a matter of sharp contention between German and Italian commanders during the course of Operation WEISS. In fact, the Italians had been requested to disarm their Chetnik auxiliaries as part of WEISS III. However, regarded as allies by the Italians, many Chetnik units were supplied with arms and ammunition and given important missions in the conduct of operations.

Since repeated requests to disarm these Chetniks were met with evasion, local German commanders were instructed to disarm and detain as prisoners any Chetniks encountered in their areas of responsibility. Strong German protests to Mussolini finally had the desired effect, and the Italian field commanders were directed to cease delivery of arms and munitions to the Chetniks and to disarm them as soon as the Partisans had been destroyed.

To forestall any repetition of the events that made necessary such a large-scale undertaking as Operation WEISS, the German Armed Forces High Command directed the Commander-in-Chief, Southeast, to retain forces in that part of Croatia just cleared of the Partisans and to secure the bauxite mines in Dalmatia, in conjunction with the Italians. The commander of German forces in the Balkans was further directed to accelerate the organization of Croatian units and to keep the matter a secret from the Italians. Presumably, these measures would provide a large number of native troops to replace German units.

However, it soon became obvious that the situation would not be improved by such measures as the expansion of the demoralized Croat police and military forces. Large concentrations of Chetniks, including those supported by the Italians, formed a constant threat to German forces in the event of an Allied landing, and the Commander-Chief, Southeast, directed that Operation SCHWARZ, under the Commander of Troops in Croatia, be undertaken in May and June to destroy the Chetniks in Herzegovina and Montenegro.

In addition to the divisions he already had assigned to him, the Commander in Croatia received the 1st Mountain Division from the Russian front and a reinforced regimental combat team of the 104th Light Division from the German forces in Serbia for the projected operation. Achieving surprise, the German forces inflicted heavy casualties on the Chetniks, capturing their commander in Montenegro, Major Djurisic, with 4,000 men, and forcing Mihailovitch to flee back into Serbia with the battered remnants of his command. In three months of the year, 985 incidents were reported, including sabotage, attacks on native officials and police, and attacks on small German and Bulgarian troop units and installations. In a particularly unenviable position were the local officials, forced to remain in office by the Germans and regarded as collaborators by both Chetniks and Partisans. Fifty-eight were murdered during the first quarter of 1943, and 197 town halls were burned or damaged. In reprisal, in addition to burning some villages and levying fines in livestock, the occupation authorities ordered the shooting of several hundred hostages from among those arrested on suspicion of being members or supporters of the Chetnik and Partisan movements. These ruthless measures had the desired effect for a time, but could not prevent the regrouping of both Chetniks and Partisans as soon as the thinly spread German or Bulgarian forces had left a particular area.

Retaliation for attacks on the Bulgarian forces was even swifter, in many cases, than the reprisals meted out by the Germans. In one such incident, in March of 1943, 32 Bulgarians were killed and 26 wounded in an attack south of Skoplje. In their fury, the Bulgarian troops shot 288 persons in the vicinity, burned 550 houses, and placed 715 person under arrest. The readiness of the Bulgarians to shoot suspects without investigation of any kind finally prompted the German Commander in Serbia to request a careful preliminary examination of each case before an execution was carried out.

II. Greece

Receiving supplies and equipment by air through the 12 British liaison officers assigned by the British Middle East forces, the EDES organization had expanded from the 98 men with which it had commenced operations in 1942 to some 600 men two months later. This growth was accelerated by British broadcasts to Greece and the award of a high British decoration to the EDES commander. The rapid growth of the force soon made it necessary to form a provisional battalion.

By March 1943, some 4,000 strong, EDES found it necessary to form more battalions and several regiments, some of which were commanded by former Greek Army officers. By July 1943, EDES had 8 to 10 units of two regiments each, the regiments each consisting of 2 battalions, and a total strength of 7,000 men. The headquarters and bulk of these forces were located in Epirus, and smaller groups operated in Thessaly and the Peloponnesus.

ELAS, leaderless until Sarafis assumed command in May 1943, WBS restricted to that time to a series of uncoordinated attacks. Under its new commander, however, ELAS soon emerged as an organized force. With an estimated seven divisions and 12,000 men by mid-1943, ELAS units were active the length of Greece, with the exception of the Pindus Mountains area, held by EDES.

The initial successes of the guerrillas against the occupation forces in 1943 were brought to an abrupt end when the German 1st Mountain Division moved from Serbia into Greece and Albania in June to bolster the Italian effort. The guerrillas, with ample warning by their excellent intelligence system, planned a heavy blow against the new enemy before he could establish himself in his occupation role.

The guerrilla operation was to be launched as the mountain troops moved south through the village of Leskovic, high in the mountains along the Greek-Albanian frontier, on the Albanian side. At that time, however, the border was crossed at will by local inhabitants, and the operation was primarily a Greek undertaking. As was their custom, the guerrillas cleared the village of all inhabitants, then placed their own men in position in the buildings along the main street. Their plan was to allow the advance guard to pass, and then to fire on the main body when the troops were confined to the street and roadway. A large force of guerrillas would then emerge from hiding places in the hills nearby to complete the destruction of the demoralized Germans.

Instead of marching blindly into the village, however, the Germans first enveloped it from either flank, and a number of the guerrillas opened fire prematurely. Deploying rapidly, the main body of the mountain troops surrounded Leskovic and shelled it thoroughly before launching their assault. The guerrilla force in hiding outside the village was routed by artillery fire when it attempted to relieve the ambushers, and Leskovic was reduced in a house-to-house operation. The stone construction of the houses afforded considerable protection to the besieged guerrillas, who inflicted heavy casualties on the mountain troops before the latter could bring a sufficient number of infantry and antitank guns into action to batter down their positions.

A number of the irregulars escaped by posing as fleeing civilians while the battle was at its height. When the Germans recognized their opponents at close range, however, they halted everyone attempting to leave the village, and soon held a motley collection of ragged men and youths. Examinations of these prisoners and of the bodies found in the rubble of Leskovic revealed most of the guerrillas to have been in civilian clothing or parts of German and Italian uniforms, with their only insignia a small hammer and sickle. The aggressive attitude of the new occupation troops, with their heavier firepower and greater battle experience, soon discouraged such ventures as the attack at Leskovic, and for a time EDES also ceased all active operations against them. However, in deference to the British Middle East forces, Zervas could not openly accept the German offer of a truce. ELAS, on the other hand, persisted with small-scale attacks on individuals and small parties.

III. The German Situation by Mid-1943

With both Yugoslav and Greek guerrillas withdrawn from large-scale operations for the moment, the Germans hastened to take steps to secure the Balkans against a threatening Italian collapse or surrender. Arrangements were made to replace Italian garrisons with German troops, and German forces were disposed in locations from which they could move quickly to contest Allied landings. As directed by the new chief of the Supreme General Staff, Generale D'Armata (General) Vittorio Ambrosio, Italian units were to withdraw without delay, ostensibly for the defense of Italy against a threatening Anglo-American invasion. In many cases, Italian units left their assigned areas before the arrival of their German relief, and the Germans had to drive out infiltrating guerrillas before occupying their new positions.

Various expedients were attempted by the Germans in an effort to fill the power vacuum the Italian withdrawal was causing. One such measure was the westward extension of the Bulgarian occupation zones in Greece and Yugoslavia. However, the certain resentment of the population and the refusal of King Boris to move Bulgarian troops farther away from the Turkish-Bulgarian border made necessary the cancellation of these plans. Deeply concerned about the possibility of Turkey's entering the war on the Allied side, the Bulgarians kept idle major forces of first-line troops while sending second-rate divisions of older reservists to garrison their zones of Greece and Yugoslavia.

Nor was the reorganization of the Croat Army and security forces of any avail. Except for the Legion troops under German command, the Croatian military and security forces were confined to the larger centers of population. Desertions became more frequent, and even Legion troops could no longer be depended upon for missions not including a hard core of German units.

It was obvious that more German troops would be required if the Balkans were to be held. Temporarily, it would suffice to have satellite and puppet military and security forces hold the interior while German units moved to the coastal areas and likely invasion points. However, it would eventually be necessary to have reliable and combat experienced troops to replace the puppet units or to furnished a cadre to stiffen them in operations. Accordingly, plans were made to strengthen the German forces by the induction of more ethnic Germans, by organizing several new divisions, and by bringing in a number of divisions and higher commands from other fronts and from German-occupied Europe.

By late June the 1st Panzer Division had arrived from France, where it had refitted after commitment on the northern and central Russian fronts. The newly formed LXVIII Corps headquarters, in army group reserve, was assigned the 1st Panzer and 117th Light Divisions, and given the mission of defending the Peloponnesus. Two other divisions were in the process of formation, the 100th Light Division in Croatia and the 297th Infantry Division in Serbia.. Additional Bulgarian troops also arrived, to bring the number of Bulgarian divisions in the occupied Balkans to seven.

As of the end of June, the Germans had a total of three Bulgarian, one Italian, and 12 of their own divisions scattered throughout those areas of the Balkans under nominal German control. Several separate regiments and security battalions, the Russian Guard Corps, and a number of coastal defense battalions and supporting units were also available, though most were of limited combat potential. The Germans planned to commit their Croatian and Serbian puppet and security troops only in an auxiliary role.

The population of the areas held by the Germans, their weakening Italian allies, the Bulgarians, and the Pavelitch government totaled almost twenty-five million persons. In Greece, the occupiers were opposed by ELAS and EDES forces estimated at 18,000 to 20,000 men; in Yugoslavia by 50,000 to 60,000 Partisans, and 12,000 to 15,000 Chetniks (mobile units only); in Albania, by a total estimated to be as many as 20,000, with the strongest group that of the Communist leader, Enver Hoxha. Many excesses of the occupation troops, particularly of the Cront Ustascha, had alienated large segments of the population. This changing attitude was promptly exploited by the guerrilla leaders, particularly the communists, who adopted a nationalist and popular front appeal to gain sympathy and support. Many former collaborationists were forgiven and accepted into the guerrilla bands, their ranks further swelled by Italian and Bulgarian deserters.

Eventual Allied victory had also become more obvious to the mass of the Balkan population by mid-1943, and few desired to be associated with a losing cause and reprisals. The judicious use of gold by the Allied liaison teams had brought a number of independent mountaineer chieftains into the guerrilla camp, and the promise of weapons secured the loyalty of many clans in the more remote regions.

The successful Allied lodgment in Sicily on 10 July and the worsening internal situation in the Balkans again raised the specter of enemy landings along the Adriatic, on the Aegean islands, or against the western coast of Greece. Accordingly, the German Armed Forces High Command, on 26 July, issued Directive No. 48, introducing major organizational changes and centralizing authority for the defense of the entire Balkan Peninsula. Generalfeldmarschall (Field Marshal) Maximilian von Weichs, formerly commander of Army Group B in southern Russia, became Commander-in-Chief, Southeast, replacing General Loehr, whose Army Group E was now restricted to Greece and the Greek islands. Marshal von Weichs, with headquarters at Belgrade, also directly commanded Army Group F, controlling all occupational troops in Yugoslavia and Albania.

One issue with the Italians was settled, at least temporarily, by the inclusion of the Italian Eleventh Army under the German theater command. In turn, the German LXVIII Corps, replacing the Italian VIII Corps on the Peloponnesus, came under control of Eleventh Army. Also, German forces in areas occupied by the Italians were placed under Italian command for tactical purposes.

Like similar directives issued earlier, the primary mission assigned the new Commander-in-Chief, Southeast, was to prepare the coastal defense of the Greek islands and mainland. To secure his rear area while so engaged and to prevent the disruption of his supply line and the movement of reinforcements in the event of Allied landings, he was further directed to destroy the guerrilla forces operating the length of the peninsula.

A mobile task force of 2 armored, 2 mountain, and 2 light infantry divisions was to be concentrated along the rail line south of Belgrade In addition to securing the most sensitive section of the Belgrade-Athens line, this centrally located force would be available for commitment against any major beachhead the Allies might succeed in effecting.

The Bulgarian 7th Infantry Division in Thrace was attached to the German command at Salonika, and the Bulgarian corps would come under German control in the event of an Allied landing. All German civilian and government agencies, with the exception of the two chief representatives of the Foreign Office, also became subordinate to the Commander-in-Chief, Southeast.

Measures to effect a more thorough reorganization of the German forces in Greece and Yugoslavia and to complete the transposition of some headquarters from administrative (territorial) to tactical status followed Directive 48. The headquarters of the XXII Mountain Corps was formed from a part of the personnel from the headquarters of the Military Commander, Southern Greece; the functions of this area commander were absorbed by the new Military Commander, Greece, whose headquarters was formed from the remaining personnel. The headquarters in Serbia was disbanded, the personnel being used to form the headquarters of the XXI Mountain Corps, assigned to Albania, and the Military Command, Southeast. A third corps head quarters, the XV Mountain, was formed from personnel of the headquarters of the Commander of German Troops in Croatia; General Lueters assumed command of the new corps with many of his old staff.

Other corps headquarters formed at the time or moved into the area included the III SS Corps, V SS Mountain Corps, and the LI and LXIX Corps. One higher headquarters, that of Second Panzer Army, arrived from the Soviet Union and established its headquarters at Kragujevac, its mission to control the large mobile force to be formed in this central Balkan area south of Belgrade and to act as a mobile reserve to counter any Allied landings in force.

A number of small-scale operations were carried out against both Partisans and Chetniks throughout Yugoslavia during this period. In contrast to large-scale operations, these had the advantage of making easier the security of preparations and the achieving of surprise, and succeeded in keeping the irregulars constantly on the move. However, they had the disadvantage of allowing individual Partisans and Chetniks to slip through repeated encirclements and escape into areas recently combed by other units or where the occupation troops were not so active at the moment.

With the Italian ally about to join the enemy, the Commander-in-Chief, Southeast, was faced with the problem of holding extensive and rebellious areas with inadequate forces, while securing a long and exposed sea flank against an enemy having overwhelming naval and air superiority. Taking advantage of the situation, Partisan units became active in the Sarajevo area; in Albania, troops of the 100th Light Division had to be committed against guerrillas who had seized control of the Tirana airfield and were effectively blocking the landing of much-needed German reinforcements by air.

CHAPTER 8

THE DEFECTION OF ITALY AND ITS EFFECTS

I. General

Italian strength in Albania, Greece, and Yugoslavia comprised thirty-one division-sized units, the bulk of them under the Italian Army Group East in Tirana, and a total of 380,000 men at the time of the signing of the Italian armistice on 3 September 1943. Though in the process of withdrawing from the Balkans at the time their government capitulated and realigned itself on the side of the Allies, these forces still held most of Albania; portions of Slovenia, Dalmatia, and Montenegro; the Ionian Coast and Islands of Greece; and a number of the Aegean Islands. In addition, they had troops in Croatia, in the interior of Greece, and under German command on Crete.

Negotiations between the Allies and the Badoglio government were conducted in great secrecy, thus the abrupt capitulation of Italy caught both Italian and German commanders by surprise. The immediate German reaction was to put Operation KONSTANTIN (seizing control of the Italian-occupied areas) into effect, and to disarm those Italian units that refused to continue the war on the German side. The capture of Foggia, with its great air base, and the adjacent ports in Italy by the Allies on 17 September made it imperative for the Germans to secure control of the Dalmatian coast and ports without delay. Unable to advance farther in Italy for the moment, the Allies might well attempt a crossing of the Adriatic in force.

The opportunity to procure much-needed weapons and equipment was not lost by the guerrillas, who immediately called upon the Italian garrisons to surrender. Fearful of guerrilla vengeance, however many Italian units waited in place to be disarmed by the Germans, and the situation developed into a race between Germans and guerrillas to reach them.

II. Yugoslavia and Albania

Some 4,000 men of the Isonzo, Bergamo, and Zara Divisions in Dalmatia, Slovenia, and Croatia deserted their units to join the Partisans and Chetniks when the Italian armistice was announced. The Firenze Division, under its commander, went over as a unit to the guerrillas in Albania. A number of higher commanders and staffs managed to obtain transportation by air or sea to Italy, while the remaining Italian troops were disarmed by the Germans and guerrillas. Incensed by what they considered treachery on the part of their former allies, the Germans made it a point to single out Italian units and installations in their continuing anti-guerrilla operations. Italian troops disarmed by the irregulars were bombed and strafed in their unit areas by German airmen, and German ground troops hunted down Italian groups and units with the guerrilla forces opposing them.

The Dalmatian port of Split, with enormous stocks of food, clothing, fuel, and ammunition for the Italian occupation forces fell to the Partisans and their thousands of adherents among the dock workers and left-wing elements of the population. Though the Partisans were forced to evacuate Split, they managed to remove considerable quantities of stores before the arrival of German forces. Nor were the Chetniks idle during this period of changing authority Strong detachments moved into Dalmatia, seizing long stretches of the coastal areas and obtaining stocks of arms from Italian' units sympathetic to them in the past.

The Croatian state, truncated by the Italian annexation of Dalmatia, moved forces into the coastal areas, fearing the Italians would try to hold Dalmatia until confirmed in its possession by the Allies as part of the reward for changing allegiance. Too, the Poglavnik had to impress his restless

population, and a show of force against the former Italian
overlords in their weakened state appeared to be an ideal
opportunity.

'The confused situation and sporadic fighting of the next few
weeks ended with the Germans in control of the ports, main
centers of population, and exposed coastal areas. The Partisans,
laden with loot, were busily re-equiping and regrouping their
forces in the mountains and carrying out a harrassing campaign
against the new occupation troops. In Slovenia and Dalmatia, to
relieve their own troops of many routine security duties, the
Germans banded together the Italian-sponsored "White Guard"
of Rupnik and the "Blue Guard" of Novak, the latter a Chetnik
commander, into the "Domobran," a home guard-type of
organization. Large numbers of Chetniks turned to the Partisans,
and others gave up the struggle to return to their homes. The
Croat units came under German control or returned to Croatia
to support the weakening government of Ante Pavelitch.

III. Greece

Farther away from home than the troops in Yugoslavia,
thousands of Italians in Greece chose to surrender to the
Germans rather than continue the war on the German side, and
numerous Italian troops from other units were integrated into
labor battalions. Unlike their countrymen in Yugoslavia, most of
the remaining Italian troops in Greece were disarmed by the
Germans and immediately interned.

Several major units, however, elected to aline themselves on
the Allied side. The Pinerolo Division and Aosta Cavalry
Regiment went over to the ELAS-EDES forces, and plans were
made to commit them as units. When one proposed operation
was refused by the Italians and another was complete]v
unsuccessful, the Greeks disarmed both the division and the
regiment and accepted volunteers from them into regular
guerrilla units. A few of the Italian troops in Greece managed to

make their way back to Italy or fled to the mountains as individuals or in small groups eventually to be captured by the guerrillas or to join the bands on their own initiative. A force of 1,100, war-weary and not desirous of fighting on either site, made its way to internment in central Turkey. The situation on the Greek islands presented a different picture to that on the mainland. While Italian forces on Crete were disarmed without difficulty by the Germans, those on Rhodes surrendered only after a pitched battle and a strong show of force. On Cephalonia, the commander and 4,000 of the garrison were shot for resisting a German demand to surrender and units on other islands established contact with British forces in the Middle East by radio to request reinforcements.

Augmented by British troops, the garrison of Leros held out against heavy German attacks for several months finally surrendering with 5,350 Italians and 3,200 British on 17 November. Samos, the last of the larger Greek islands held by the Italians, surrendered a days later.

It was proposed by some planners that the Germans abandon the southern part of the Balkan Peninsula and withdraw to a more defensible line in northern Greece. Hitler, however, would not permit it, nor could Germany risk exposing; the sources of so many strategic raw materials to attack by aircraft the Allies would certainly bring with them to Greek bases. An estimated 50 percent of Germany's oil, all of its chrome, 60 percent of its bauxite, 24 percent of its antimony, and 21 percent of its copper were procured from Balkan sources. Hence, despite the advance of Allied troops in Italy to a point below Rome and the superiority of the Allied air forces over southern Greece and the Greek islands, the German defenders were ordered to remain in place.

CHAPTER 9

OPERATIONS TO THE END OF 1943

I. General

Exhausted by long marches and intermittent fighting to gain the areas vacated by the Italians, the German troops were in no condition to pursue the guerrillas into the mountains. Instead, German commanders flurried to set up a defense against Allied landings, allocated units specific areas of responsibility, and organized mobile forces to seek out and destroy the guerrilla bands.

Experience already gained in operations in the Balkans and in Russia enabled the Germans to devise more effective anti-guerilla measures than had their Italian predecessors. With the forces at hand, they set out to contain the guerillas and keep up the flow of bauxite and other strategic raw materials produced in the Balkans to the German war machine. On the passive defense side, the occupiers set up a network of tuetzpunkte (strongpoints) to secure vital rail and road arteries and important installations. These strongpoints were actually small forts, heavily armed with automatic weapons, mortars, antitank guns, and even light field pieces, and situated in the vicinity of such guerrilla targets as bridges, tunnels, and portions of the rail and road lines difficult to keep under observation from the air or by roving patrols. Strongpoints were first occupied by a minimum of one squad, later by a platoon, when the smaller garrisons began to invite attack by the increasingly aggressive enemy. Some were of the field type with earthen trenches and bunkers reinforced and revested with logs and sandbags; others were elaborately   constructed   concrete   fortifications   with accommodations for a permanent garrison. They were Situated to deliver all-round fire, and usually had radio communication with the next higher headquarters and adjacent strongpoints. Approaches to the positions were heavily mined, and the lanes through the mine fields were changed frequently. Barbed wire obstacles were also constructed, but were seldom effective against determined attackers Armored car patrols, R platoon or more in strength and equipped with searchlights and heavy weapons, made frequently armed irregular runs between strongpoints; the same was done with armored trains along the vulnerable rail lines. In addition, mobile and heavily armed reserves, ready to move immediately to the relief of strongpoints under attack.

Personnel limitations made it necessary to place strongpoints an average of 6 miles or more apart, requiring long patrols even on the main highways. The guerrillas were quick to take advantage of the situation and made extensive use of a pressure-type mine apparently supplied by the Western Allies or Russians. Disguised to resemble R stone, this mine had a nonmetallic casing and could not be discovered readily even with a mine detector. Placed on the rock-strewn mountain roads, the mine disabled numerous vehicles' leaving the German crews afoot and at the mercy of the roving guerrillas. Other devices put to extensive use were land mines, demolitions, and special nails designed to puncture tires. The last, easily transportable, could be dropped along the road at frequent intervals by shepherds moving their flocks from one grazing area to another.

A highly effective offensive weapon was found in the Jagdkommando (ranger detachment), designed to seek out and destroy guerrilla bands. Personnel of the detachments were usually young and combatwise veterans of German campaigns on other fronts. Physically hardy and trained to live in the open for extended periods of time, they depended little on supply columns and could pursue the guerrillas, often burdened down with wounded, families. and impedimenta, into the most inaccessible areas. When the situation required, the rangers would put on civilian clothing, disguising themselves as Chetniks or Partisans, to work their way closer to their wary enemy. In the event they came upon major guerrilla forces, the ranger detachments, seldom more than a company in strength, would keep them under observation and inform battalion or other higher headquarters. While awaiting reinforcements, they would attempt to gather additional information on the guerrilla strength and dispositions. As successful as they were in many small-scale operations; however, the ranger detachments were not numerous enough to affect decisively the outcome of the antiguerrilla campaign.

A directive from the German Armed Forces High Command on 19 September made Generalfeldmarschall (Field Marshal) Rommel and Army Group B, in conjunction with the Commander-in-Chief, Southeast, responsible for destroying the large guerrilla forces on the Istrian Peninsula bordering Croatia. Further, to strengthen the German Forces in the Balkans, the Commander-in-Chief, South, was to turn over to Marshal von Weichs all captured tanks and other armored vehicles unsuitable for use against the Allies in Italy. This ambitious plan to eliminate the guerrilla scourge in northwest Yugoslavia and the Yugoslav-Italian border area, and a contemplated transfer of several divisions from Army Group B to the Commander-in-Chief. Southeast, was thwarted by developments in Italy and the departure of Marshal Rommel and his staff to France. Marshal von Weichs also lost the 1st Panzer Division, ordered to the Russian front in August.

German forces continued to move into the Balkans in the month following the defection of the Italians. By the end of September 1943, the number of German divisions had increased to 14. Total strength was approximately 600,000 military personnel, a serious drain on the Reich's dwindling manpower resources. Opposing them, the Germans estimated the rapidly growing guerrilla forces in the theater at 145,000, the bulk of them, some 90,000, under Tito's command.

By early November the German forces in the Balkans comprised 17 divisions. The Armed Forces High Command then directed a search of all cities and centers of population in the Balkan Peninsula as a preliminary to major operations to destroy the guerrillas. Despite the strenuous objections of the theater commander, who protested the personnel available to him were far too few, the search operation was carried out on schedule, but with completely unsatisfactory results.

The Bulgarians also became a problem during November, with whole units disaffected by communist agitators. On one occasion, the 24th Bulgarian Division had to be withdrawn from an operation against the Partisans when it refused to obey the orders of the German task force commander. Desertions to the guerrillas became more frequent, and several communist bands of Bulgarian deserters were organized to operate against German forces and their own government in southern and western Bulgaria from bases on Yugoslav soil. By the end of the year, German troop strength had climbed to 700,000 men total of 20 Infantry, SS, and mountain divisions Despite this impressive total, however, and the attention the that was receiving from the Armed Forces High Command, the southeast still held a secondary place in order of priority. Troop replacements were invariably older men or those returned to duty after long periods in the hospital. Vehicles, including tanks, were often obsolescent or war booty from the 1940 campaign in western Europe.

II. Yugoslavia and Albania

Major anti-Partisan operations planned for late 1943 included KUGELBLITZ, SCHNEESTURM, and HERBSTGEWITTER. The first of these, executed by the V SS Mountain Corps, had as its purpose the destruction of the Partisan units in eastern Bosnia.

Marshal Tito during the Second World War in Yugoslavia, May 1944

The German troop units had to comb too large an area to be thorough, however, and the bulk of the Partisan force slipped through their narrowing ring. The Partisans suffered 9,000 casualties in the course of the operation, and were immediately pursued in Operation SCHNEESTURM, twin drives to the west and northwest. Concluded by the end of December, SCHNEESTURM cost the Partisans an additional 2,000 men. Though badly battered in these operations, the major Partisan units retained their cohesion and Tito's Army of National Liberation could still be considered an effective fighting force.

HERBSTGEWITTER involved the clearing of the island of Korcula, off the Dalmatian Coast, an excellent waystation for bringing supplies in by sea from Italy. The Partisans lost 1,000 men in the operation. However, perhaps more significant than this loss was the matter of a reprisal inflicted on the Partisan garrison.

The Commander-in-Chief, Southeast, had received a report on the shooting of German officers and 26 enlisted men captured by the 29th Partisan Division near Mostar. One of the officers was a holder of the Knight's Cross of the Iron Cross (the German equivalent of the Distinguished Service Cross), which further incensed Marshal von Weichs. Accordingly, he ordered the execution of 220 prisoners from Korcula in reprisal, giving the Partisans additional ammunition for their propaganda campaign.

As of the end of the year, the headquarters of Second Panzer Army, which had arrived from Russia in August to assume control of the major striking force of Army Group F, had 14 divisions in Yugoslavia and Albania. The 367th Infantry Division, hastily formed in Germany in October, was assigned to garrison duty in Croatia while completing its organization and training. The Military Command, Southeast, had operational control over the I Bulgarian Corps in Serbia and a number of police and security units of regimental and battalion size.

It was at this time that a number of the Allied liaison officers were withdrawn from the Chetniks, and with their departure the supply of weapons and equipment from the Middle East forces and Italy was considerably reduced. With much of their portion of Allied military assistance diverted to the Partisans and under constant attack by Tito's forces, the position of the Chetniks began to deteriorate. Though they still held Serbia and some of the Adriatic coastal regions, their strength waned with battle losses and desertions.

No doubt existed as to the loyalty of Mihailovitch himself to the royal Yugoslavian Government-in-Exile. However, there is ample evidence that a number of his subordinates made armistice arrangements with the occupation forces and even assisted them on occasion. Certain the Germans and their allies would eventually be forced to withdraw from the Balkans, Mihailovitch regarded the Partisans, under the aegis of Moscow, as the greater of the two threats to the restoration of the former government

III. Greece

With its more homogeneous population and a central government, however weak and collaborationist, Greece did not pose the occupation problem that Yugoslavia did during this period. The average German had considerable respect for the culture of ancient Hellas, and was better disposed toward the Greek population than toward the various Yugoslav peoples, whom he regarded as offshoots of the Russians and Slavic barbarians. Too, the economic situation in Greece, unable to raise enough food to sustain even its own population and reduced to abject poverty by the complete loss of its world-wide foreign trade of prewar years, did much to keep the Greeks under the control old the occupation forces and the puppet regime.

Major operations undertaken by the Germans during the period were the clearing of the Edessa-Florina road, west of Salonika, accomplished in conjunction with Bulgarian forces moved west for the purpose, and PANTHER, the elimination of guerrilla bands in the Metsovan Pass, Yannina-Arta, and Mount Olympus areas. In the Edessa-Florina operation, the guerrilla forces melted away into the mountains, and neither side sustained casualties comparable to those suffered in the fighting in Yugoslavia. In Operation PANTHER, the guerrillas lost 1,400 men, 3 field pieces, and a considerable stock of small arms.

As of the end of the year, Army Group E had attached to it the XXII Mountain and LXVIII Corps, the former responsible for western Greece and the Peloponnesus and the latter for eastern Greece. In addition, Fortress Crete, raised to corps status and no longer under the theater headquarters, was directly responsible to the army group commander. A total of 6 divisions, 1 of them Bulgarian, formed the combat nucleus of the army group. In the event of major Allied landings, the 2 divisions from the Bulgarian corps in Thrace would also come under the control of Army Group E.

CHAPTER 10
OPERATIONS IN 1944

I. General

The Italians had been eliminated from a major role on the military scene, except for individuals and small units fighting on either side, and the Balkan occupation by the beginning of 1944 had become a heavy burden to the Germans. The Wehrmacht was bleeding to death in Russia, and the invasion of France was but a few months away; United States, British, and other Allied forces were firmly established in Italy. The Bulgarians, formerly reliable allies and assigned a responsible part in the occupation, were growing acutely concerned with the possibility of Turkey's entering the war on the Allied side; a Turkish attack through Thrace had become a nightmare to the Bulgarian leaders.

The lesser satellite and puppet forces, including the Ustascha and national army of Croatia, the Serbian State Guard and Volunteer Corps, and various Yugoslav, Greek, and Albanian security and auxiliary units, had begun to desert in increasing numbers to the Partisans and ELAS, and a few to the Chetniks and EDES. The Russian Guard Corps, as well as such Russian-German formations as the 1st Cossack Division, which had arrived in Yugoslavia in late 1943, remained loyal to the Germans. However, the dilution of the Guard Corps with former prisoners of war and the excesses of the Cossack Division against the civilian population reacted to the disadvantage of the Germans. The former prisoners, brought up in the Soviet mold, were completely alien to the older Russians, and the Guard Corps lost some of its Czarist flavor. The 1st Cossack Division, which included Kuban, Terek, Don, and Siberian Cossacks who had seen hard service against Soviet guerrillas, left a trail of burned villages and terror-stricken peasants in its wake.

The German units, however, despite this weakened support, still presented a formidable military force to the irregulars, and could march into and occupy any part of Greece, Albania, and Yugoslavia et any time, an argument often given to justify their treatment of captured guerrillas as illegal combatants. Moreover, strong and seasoned reserves were available in the 1st Mountain Division, as well as several others less well known, to be rushed to the scene of any protracted rising.

II. The Area of Army Group E

To keep as many as possible of its better-trained troops available as a mobile striking force to counter Allied landings in Greece, Army Group E had already received a number of "Eastern" battalions, composed of Russians, Ukranians, Poles, and other Slavic groups, to supplement its German security units. Too, thousands of Italians, after a few months in German internment camps, found a more tolerable existence in labor and other auxiliary units. Known to the Germans as Hiwis (Hilfswillige), the labor troops relieved combat units by building coastal fortifications, constructing strongpoints, and repairing the extensive damage done by Allied bombing, now increasing in intensity; the Kawis (Kampfwillige) assisted by performing various guard and security duties. The heterogeneous collection of foreign troops proved insufficient for the maintenance of law and order in Greece, however, and the commander of Army Group E requested and received permission to raise and equip a battalion of Greek security troops, knowing approval for more would be forthcoming if the new unit could make any substantial contribution to the German defense plan.

This pilot model was known as the Laocoon Volunteer Battalion after Laoccoon of Greek mythology, and had approximately 700 men. Arms were limited to rifles and machine guns, and the first mission of the battalion was to participate in the clearing of the Peloponnesus. The fair success attained in the operation convinced the Germans of the advisability of organizing two additional battalions.

The practice of replacing German units with foreign troops had its disadvantages, however. For example, it had become necessary for General Loehr to warn all Russian members of the Eastern battalions against desertion. The worsening German war situation had prompted Stalin to call on all Soviet citizens in German service to obstruct operations in any way they could, and a number had done so by deserting, spreading rumors, and inciting the troops against their German officers and non-commissioned officers.

Next, the general reluctance among the Italians in the German auxiliary services caused the army group commander to require an oath of allegiance from each man. A full 30 percent of the Italians refused to take the oath, and rumors were rife among the 70 percent who did that they would be called upon for front-line service. According to other rumors, each man taking the oath of allegiance in the German cause would be imprisoned for 10 years if he were ever to return to Italy. The already low morale and lukewarm support of the Italians sank to new depths when this news became general knowledge among the labor and security units.

Nor had the situation with the Bulgarians improved. Reports from the liaison officer with the II Bulgarian Corps stressed the defeatist attitude of the corps commander and his staff, who despaired of holding the Thracian coast against a determined Anglo-American landing in forces. Rather, the Bulgarians preferred to build a defense line along the Rhodope Mountains, just inside their own country. Believing an invasion would be preceded by a large-scale airborne landing to their rear, they feared the cutting of communications with the Bulgarian zone of the interior.

Respecting the Bulgarians as hardy and willing soldiers, the

Germans pointed out that the Bulgarian lack of experience in modern military operations had caused them to overestimate the Allies, and that a strong coastal defense organization would discourage any landing in an area so exposed to a German flank attack from the Greek peninsula. The Bulgarians, temporarily reassured, expanded the' construction of coastal defenses and agreed to send a number of their commanders and staff officers to observe German operations in Italy.

The German units, bearing the brunt of the anti-guerrilla effort, had difficulties of their own, chief among them a shortage of personnel. To supplement the trickle of replacements, General Loehr directed all service organizations to make their able-bodied men available for, transfer to combat units. The commander of Army Group E also had to overcome some lethargy on the part of subordinate headquarters and on one occasion sent a sternly worded directive ordering the abolishment of such terms as "Sunday duty" from the staff duty roster of the corps and area commands.

A number of operations were undertaken by units of Army Group during the opening months of 1944 in an attempt do clear guerrilla infested areas of Greece. Though not on the large scale of operations in Yugoslavia to the north, they nonetheless diverted thousands a troops from the preparation of coastal defenses and transfer to other theaters of war. In addition, they involved extensive use of vehicle. and an expenditure of gasoline the Germans could ill afford.

The first operation of significance, in the Salonika-Aegean area, was called WOLF; both German and Bulgarian troops participated. A total of 254 enemy dead was counted, and over 400 prisoners taken. Operation HORRIDO followed, with units of the XXII Mountain Corps participating. Guerrilla casualties totaled 310 dead and captured, while the German troops suffered 18 dead, wounded, and missing.

During this period the economic situation worsened steadily, with the value of the Greek drachma reduced to a point where it required 500,000 to purchase a pound of butter on the widespread black mark. As a result, large numbers of Greeks fled to join the guerrillas, particularly the communist group. General Loehr, for this reason, found necessary to direct the troops to desist from interfering with food shipments and neutral relief agencies, in the hope the gap in security his order created would be offset by an improved level of subsistence for the bulk of the population.

The Germans still had some supporters from the anti-Communist elements of the Greek population, among them EDES. For keeping the Yannina-Arta road and a large part of the Pindus Mountains area cleared of ELAS forces, EDES was supplied with small arms and ammunition by local German commanders, a practice approved by the army group commander. According to revised German estimates, Zervas' main force at this time comprised only 2,500-3,000 men, but these were well disciplined, adequately armed, and organized into properly balanced units, with sufficient heavy weapons for support in their particular type of combat. ELAS, by contrast, had grown to 20,000 men, uniformly armed only to battalion and lacking heavy weapons in sufficient numbers or the more rigid organization and discipline of Zervas' nationalists.

Started the end of February, Operation RENNTIER was concluded in March, with a total of 96 guerrilla dead and 100 prisoners. The Germans suffered 2 and the Bulgarians 7 casualties in the operation. A second operation in thc Salonika-Aegean area, with the code name ILTIS, cost the guerrillas an additional 15 men. A communist-inspired strike in the Piraeus area in March was put down by the Germans only after security troops fired on the demonstrators, killing 21; an additional 132 strikers were taken into custody. Immediately following this, a German truck column on the Sparta-Tripolis road in the Peloponnesus was attacked, and a total of 18 Germans killed and

44 wounded. In reprisal, 200 communist suspects were executed, 10 villages burned, and martial law declared throughout the Peloponnesus. Both of these events worsened relations between the Greek civilian population and the German occupiers.

Another measure taken by Army Group E was the establishment of a restricted zone on either side of the railroad lines used by the German forces. In open country, this extended to 5 kilometers (approx. 3 miles) on either side of the track; in populated areas, to 200 meters (220 yds.). Within this zone, civilians were warned, they would be fired upon on sight.

While clearing operations, restrictions on movement in the area of the rail lines, and the active assistance of EDES and the Greek volunteer battalions restored a measure of security to the German supply routes, guerrilla forces increased their activities in more remote areas. On Euboea, elements of the LXVIII Corps and Greek auxiliaries had to be committed in a clearing operation that cost the guerrillas 85 dead and 69 prisoners. A concurrent small-scale operation in the Salonika-Aegean area cost the Greek resistance forces 13 casualties and the Germans 12. Continuously engaged in operations, the occupational command for the Salonika-Aegean area became the Salonika Corps Group, and was raised to tactical corps status.

Friction again developed with the Bulgarians at this time. Contrary to the wishes of the Germans, to whom they were now subordinated tactically, the Bulgarians assigned fully a quarter of the troops of their II Corps to the task of securing the interior of Thrace, up to the mountain passes into Bulgaria. The Germans protested this weakening of the coastal garrisons, already reduced to a point where only 11 heavy batteries were left available for coast artillery support for an exposed sea front of almost 200 miles. In reply, the Bulgarians stated they considered it necessary to secure a route for reinforcements in the event of an Allied landing. Despite the dissatisfaction of Army Group E, the Bulgarians maintained their position, widening the breach in relations. The irritation grew with some activities of Bulgarian units operating in German occupied areas. Reluctant to leave after the completion of a mission, the Bulgarians frequently had to be ordered to return to their own zone. In turn, these units resented the German requirement that they turn over all weapons and booty taken in joint operations. Bulgarian minorities in German-occupied Greece also played a part in the dissension. Allowed to form home guard-type companies at the insistence of the Bulgarian II Corps, the minorities used these armed units to dominate their Greek neighbors, who in turn blamed the German authorities for placing them in such a position. Operations in early April involved the clearing of a number of mountain passes in northern Greece, a preliminary movement to Operation MAIGEWITTER, a large-scale effort to destroy ELAS forces in that part of the army group area. The total guerrilla loss in the operation was 339 dead and 75 captured, with 200 suspects arrested.

Repeated Allied commando and air raids on the Greek islands made necessary the issuance of special instructions to the captains of the small vessels making the hazardous supply runs to isolated garrisons in the Aegean and Ionian Seas areas. Gun crews were to stand by at action stations when their vessels approached island anchorages, and supplies were to be unloaded only after the garrisons had been identified. Movement was to be at night where possible, with gun crews ready for sudden air attacks even in port. The excellent intelligence net of the guerrillas and Allies made it difficult for the Germans to maintain security of ship movements, however; this was well illustrated by the sinking of a ship carrying large stocks of small arms and machine gun ammunition to Crete and other island outposts.

On several occasions British commando troops managed to remain on various Greek islands for periods of several days, making detailed reconnaissance and taking prisoners for interrogation at Middle East headquarters. Perhaps the best known of these prisoners was Generalmajor (Brigadier General) Karl Kreipe, commanding the 22d Airborne Division on Crete, and captured on 26 April by a party that penetrated the coastal defenses and succeeded in evacuating the general past a number of security outposts. This persistent Allied interest in Greece tended to keep the German occupying forces constantly on the alert, a strain on commanders, staffs, troops, and communications. The mounting number of suicides on Crete alone, from 11 in 1942 to 41 in 1943, perhaps best exemplified the slump in morale and spirit occasioned by this type of duty. The garrison of Crete was evacuated before the end of 1944, hence no figures are available for that year. However, the situation became serious enough to be called to the attention of General Loehr by his chief medical officer.

The situation in Greece became more tense during May and June. The army group commander, to provide additional armed men in the ovens of emergency, directed the conscription of all able-bodied, male Germans resident in Greece, including civilians attached to the economic and diplomatic missions, the Organization Todt (construction workers), and employees of the various armed services. Practice alerts were held frequently, and rear area troops, as well as the provisional units of new conscripts, were given intensive instruction in the use of small arms. The guerrillas, meanwhile, emboldened by the prospect of an impending German withdrawal, increased the tempo of their attacks. During the first week of May, Generalleutenant (Major General) Krech, commanding the 41st Fortress Division on the Peloponnesus was killed in a surprise attack, with 3 enlisted men of his headquarters, 325 communist suspects were shot in reprisal. Other attacks were made on German supply lines, and sabotage extended even to armed vessels at anchor in Greek harbors.

Apparently oblivious to the situation in which the German

forces in Greece now found themselves, the Armed Forces High Command, through the headquarters of Marshal von Weichs, directed the securing of the Greek sea areas and the defense of the peninsula to the last. Operation NEPTUN, later compromised and changed to KORALLE, was undertaken to clear the Sporades Islands area and adjacent waters in compliance with this order, but succeeded only in drawing superior British naval forces to the scene of battle. EINHORN, also compromised and changed to GEMSBOCK, was completed by the XXII Mountain Corps in early June; the purpose of the operation was to inflict a decisive defeat on the growing guerrilla forces in the Greek-Albanian border area. Quite successful, GEMSBOCK was followed three weeks later by Operation STEINADLER, to destroy ELAS units in the Pentalofon area. While the XXII Mountain Corps conducted GEMSBOCK in western Greece and southern Albania, the LXVIII Corps in the Peloponnesus and eastern Greece pursued several operations of its own. The results in the numbers of guerrillas killed and captured, however, were considerably less than in GEMSBOCK.

An increasing number of desertions by the Ossets, a Caucasus Mountains race well represented in the Eastern battalions, caused the army group commander to direct that all Ossets be disarmed and detained as prisoners of war. From a support to German manpower, the "Eastern" battalions now became an increasing liability. A watch also had to be kept on the Italian volunteers dispersed throughout the German security battalions in a ratio of one "company" of 40 men per battalion. Reports of disaffection among such units under German command in northern Italy caused considerable concern over the matter at army group headquarters. A number of Bulgarian volunteers serving in Wehrmacht units also had to be disarmed in June, as did part of the 814th Armenian Battalion, adding to the enormous number of prisoners of war and internees in German custody in Greece.

Early July brought a realignment of German combat strength in Greece when the 4th SS Police Division, which had then been in Greece almost a year, was alerted for movement to the north. The consequent shifting of forces made it necessary for the 41st Fortress Division, a static unit composed in large part of former general military prisoners, to take over the defense of the entire Peloponnesus. The 11th Luftwaffe Field Division, in Attica, was given an added area of responsibility, which included Thessaly, infested by ELAS and EKKA forces. Units of the air force field division lost control of much of the area to the guerrillas in a matter of days, and had difficulty maintaining the major north-south roads and rail lines.

On 3 July EDES abruptly reopened hostilities with the occupation forces, seizing 10 kilometers (6.5 miles) of coastline in the vicinity of Parga. Two days later, during the night of 5-6 July, EDES forces attacked German troops in the vicinity of Arta. To defend themselves, the Germans undertook several small-scale countermoves, meanwhile trying to determine the intentions of Zervas prior to any major offensive to eliminate him. Intelligence reports at first supported the theory that British liaison officers had seized command of the Zervas organization, in conjunction with a group of anti-German commanders led by Colonel Kamaras of the 10th EDES Division. Later, several clandestine meetings between Zervas and representatives of the German forces made it obvious that the Greek leader had been influenced by the Allied liaison mission to renege on his agreement with the occupation forces. The coastal area Zervas had seized, with its easy access to the EDES-controlled Pindus Mountains, permitted the landing of 5,000 reinforcements from the Greek units under British command in Egypt. These units were immediately distributed throughout the Zervas organization and represented a substantial increase in effective troop strength.

Since a reinforced and hostile EDES represented a threat to his forces, the commander of Army Group E directed the destruction of the Zervas organization after the completion of Operation STEINADLER. General Loehr also directed additional changes in coastal defense, based on German experiences in the Normandy operation. Beach defenses were to be manned only by troops of the static fortress battalions, while the reduced mobile forces of the 104th Light and other divisions were to be assembled in areas to the rear to counter Allied landings.

The offensive against EDES, for which the already alerted 4th SS Division was made available, was the responsibility of the XXII Mountain Corps. Called by the code name of KREUZOTTER, the operation, beginning 5 August, was only moderately successful. EDES lost a total of 298 dead and 260 prisoners, as against German casualties of 20 dead, 112 wounded, and one missing.

More important events, on the international scene, soon eclipsed antiguerrilla operations in the area of Army Group E. The Romanians surrendered to the advancing Russians on 24 August, and Soviet forces were perilously close to the Bulgarian frontier. Though not at war with the Soviet Union, the Bulgarians feared imminent invasion by either Russians or Turks, and government leaders met to consider ending the alliance with Germany. As a result, orders were given Bulgarian frontier troops to disarm German units withdrawing from Romania, and the II Corps, in Thrace, was directed to prepare for movement home during the first week in September. The German liaison missions with higher Bulgarian headquarters remained on in their assignments, however, and Wehrmacht units scattered throughout Thrace and in Bulgaria itself organized themselves into small combat groups to resist any attempt by the Bulgarians to disarm them. Hitler, furious at what he considered Bulgarian duplicity, ordered all German troops moving into Bulgaria to remain under arms and all units to defend their positions in Bulgaria and Bulgarian-occupied areas to the last cartridge (an order now somewhat timeworn in the Fuehrer's directives to his field commanders).

Among the troops and commanders, German-Bulgarian relations remained amicable enough. In evacuating the coastal area, Bulgarian artillery units left their immobile pieces in position for German crews to man, and the German liaison officer to the II Corps was allowed to maintain contact with the headquarters of Army Group E. Individuals and small parties outside their respective zones were allowed to return to their units unmolested.

While resigned to the loss of Thrace, the Bulgarian Government, despite the imminent crisis with the Soviet Union, had no intention of relinquishing its status in Yugoslavia. Accordingly, since it lay directly across the main axis of communications between Army Group E and German headquarters for all the southeast at Belgrade, it was necessary for the Germans to make plans to secure Yugoslav Macedonia and southeastern Serbia the former occupied by the Bulgarian V Corps and the latter by the I Corps. Plan TREUBRUCH assigned the 1st Mountain Division the mission of seizing Skopje, largest city and rail center of the area; Plan HUNDESSOHN involved the movement of the 4th SS Police Division into Bulgaria in the direction of Sofiya, the capital; Plan JUDAS was the disarmament of the Bulgarian forces in Thrace and Macedonia. Arrangements were made with Army Group F for units of Army Group E to move into its area of responsibility.

While German units prepared for their respective parts in the operations planned in event of hostilities with Bulgaria, fighting with the guerrilla forces increased in intensity. For the 2-month period ending in August, the Germans suffered a total of 936 dead, 1,235 wounded, and 275 missing, meanwhile inflicting casualties on the guerrillas amount to 5,394 dead and 768 captured. Personnel casualties in air attacks on trains, convoys, and troop areas also reached a high during this period, with 32 dead and 26 wounded for the week ending 4 August alone. To improve the air defense of their rail lines and installations, Luftwaffe units were directed to fly high over the railroads and to avoid flying parallel to them. Antiaircraft crews and troops defending the trains and lines were then free to open fire on any aircraft approaching at a low altitude.

The situation by the end of August made it necessary for Army Group E to order the evacuation of all troops in Greece, with the exception of the garrisons of Crete and Rhodes, to the area north of the line Corfu-Yannina-Kalabaka-Olympus. The withdrawal was to be orderly, and measures taken to prevent German intentions becoming known to the Greek population. The troops on railroad security duty were reinforced, and Corps Group Salonika, a provisional organization formed from the administrative command for the Salonika-Aegean area, was merged with an existing skeletal staff to form the XCI Corps headquarters and control units in the Salonika region, through which all forces from the south would have to pass.

On 8 September, Bulgaria declared war on Germany and immediately dispatched strong forces from Sofiya in the direction of the Yugoslav frontier. Lacking the strength to put their ambitious HUNDESSOHN and JUDAS plans into effect, the Germans hurried the 1st Mountain Division to Skoplje, where it operated temporarily under control of the Second Panzer Army, to implement Plan TREUBRUCH. While 5,000 Bulgarians at Bitolj laid down their arms after a brief show of resistance, the garrison at Prilep and Bulgarian units in the Skoplje area fought stubbornly. However, the 1st Mountain Division eventually managed to seize and hold the city of Skoplje and the vital railroad along the Vardar River. Bulgarian units bypassed in the fast German move to the north succeeded in breaking the line at a number of points and had to be driven off by combat groups formed from troops moving northward from Greece to join the 1st Mountain Division.

On the night of 9 September, a general rising made it obvious that German units below the line Corfu-Yannina-Kalabaka-Olympus would have to fight their way north. Moving down from the mountains in force, both ELAS and EDES attempted to block the major roads and railways to the north. In western Greece, troops of the XXII Mountain Corps had to fight hard to keep the Arta-Yannina road open in order to evacuate the Cephalonia garrison and units in southwestern Greece. In eastern Greece, the LXVIII Reserve Corps, having already lost its 11th Luftwaffe Field Division to the defense of Macedonia, managed to regain long stretches of the rail line to Salonika only after a series of seesaw actions with strong ELAS units.

To reinforce the units already heavily engaged in the north and threatened by an estimated three Bulgarian armies moving west to cut off the withdrawal of Army Group E, General Loehr directed an airlift of combat troops from Crete and Rhodes. A total of 11,500 men evacuated from Crete alone in this operation, most of them from the 22d Airborne Division, proved to be a substantial addition to the hard-pressed units north of Salonika. However, fighter aircraft from Allied carriers now operating in force in Greek waters made impossible the completion of the airlift. As of 12 October, some 26,500 service and combat troops were still stranded on Crete, Rhodes, and other German-held islands, with little or no prospect of escape. Instructed to fight to the end and destroy all installations and materiel of value to the enemy, the bulk of these troops, representing all three services, were left to their fate.

Its success in holding open the route of withdrawal to the north could not obscure the fact that Army Group E was in a difficult position. All available troops had been thrown into the fighting against the Russians and Bulgarians along a line roughly paralleling the southeastern Yugoslav border. In the rear areas in Yugoslav Macedonia, Albanian guerrillas and Partisan units roamed almost at will off the main roads and rail lines, and the

Partisans had established contact with Bulgarian irregulars operating with their own army as reconnaissance and screening forces. Accordingly, Army Group E directed the complete evacuation of Greece and the establishment of a new defense along the line Scutari-Skoplje-Negotin. On 14 October headquarters of Army Group E moved to Yugoslav Macedonia, where it estimated it had the equivalent of four German divisions holding a line of 375 miles against 13.5 Soviet and Bulgarian divisions. While the rugged country allowed them to confine their efforts to holding the mountain passes and other avenues of approach, this advantage was more than offset by the German inferiority in numbers and lack of air support and by the activities of the guerrillas. Information from prisoners revealed the Third Ukrainian Front (Army Group) to be in Sofiya directing operations, with the Thirty Seventh and Fifty Seventh Soviet Armies under its control. The Bulgarian armies were the First, Second, and Fourth. The use of Stuka aircraft by the Bulgarians, who had obtained them under the Axis equivalent of lend-lease during the period of the alliance-with Germany, was particularly exasperating to the troops of Army Group E.

The few units still remaining in Greece, comprising mostly supply and other service troops, now found themselves in a position similar to that of the island garrisons. Lacking adequate transportation and the fire-power of combat units, these troops were ordered to fight to the last and to destroy all stocks and equipment of any value to the guerrillas. While some carried out the destruction as ordered, in a number of cases installation commanders turned critically needed food, medicines, and clothing over to agencies of the Greek Government.

As British troops landed in southern Greece and the occupation rapidly approached its end, ELAS and EDES became engaged in a civil war that prevented both them and the British from participating in the pursuit of the Germans. On 2 November the last organized German units to evacuate Greece crossed the border into Yugoslavia, and German control of Greece was history.

III. The Area of Army Group F

The German command structure in Yugoslavia as of the first of the year was an anomaly. Army Group F, which controlled all German forces in Yugoslavia and Albania, was also Supreme Headquarters, Southeast. As Commander-in-Chief, Southeast, Marshal von Weichs controlled Army Group E as well, in effect placing Army Group F in the position of being the headquarters to which Army Group E was responsible.

As subordinate commands in Yugoslavia and Albania, Army Group F had the Second Panzer Army, with headquarters at Kragujevac, and the Military Command, Southeast, with headquarters at Belgrade. Actually, the titles of both headquarters were inaccurate, since the Second Panzer Army had no armored divisions at the time and but one or two tank battalions as army troops, while the Military Commander, Southeast, was the area commander in Serbia, and commanded the tactical troops in the area in the dual role of Army Commander, Serbia. Although the Second Panzer Army retained its designation until the end, it might have been more properly called the Second Mountain Army. Attached to these two commands and Army Group F were the I Bulgarian Corps of four divisions; four German corps, with eleven infantry, one cavalry (Cossack), one mountain, and one SS mountain division; and army and army group troops.

Facing a better-armed and more numerous enemy than the German forces in Greece, Army Group F was all but forced on the defensive in the opening months of 1944. While the Chetniks still maintained an uneasy peace, the Partisans had grown to a force able to hold a large area of the country by themselves, including even transportation and communications facilities, and to set up a provisional government. Small-scale operations by the various divisions and smaller units met with some success, but the center of the Partisan movement, in the Enin-Jajce-Bihac-Banja Luka area, remained a refuge to which Tito's units could withdraw when German pressure became too great in any other particular area. Accordingly, to regain the initiative now all but lost, and to strike the Partisans a blow from which they would not soon recover, Marshal von Weichs ordered the Second Panzer Army to destroy the Tito forces in their main stronghold. The operation was known as ROESSELSPRUNG, and it was planned to commit elements of the 1st Mountain Division, elements of the Division Brandenburg (designation of a special demolitions and sabotage unit), the 202d Tank Battalion, the 92d Motorized Infantry Regiment (Separate), an SS parachute battalion, and a number of Croatian units.

The parachutists and glider troops were dropped on Tito's headquarters at Dvar on 25 May, while tank and infantry units converged from Bihac, Banja Luka, and Livno. Though Tito himself managed to escape, the Partisan headquarters was captured, with its extensive communications system. The 1st and 6th Partisan Divisions were badly mauled in the fighting, suffering a total of 6,000 casualties, and an enormous stock of booty taken. Though not a fatal blow, the operation did achieve its purpose in that the Partisan chain of command was temporarily broken until Tito could establish himself on the island of Vis under British protection, and the heavy personnel and materiel losses forced the guerrillas to withdraw from operations in the area to reorganize and regroup. The German satisfaction over the results of the operation was somewhat tempered,- however, with the losses inflicted on the attackers when United States and British aircraft surprised them in the process of combing and clearing the Hvar area.

Strong concentrations of Partisans in Montenegro made it necessary to plan another large-scale operation, called RUEBEZAHL. However, before RUEBEZAHL could be launched, the movement of Partisans toward the Macedonia region required immediate and effective action. Aware of the impending German withdrawal from Greece and the Soviet advance to the west, the Partisans rushed the first of an estimated thirteen divisions in the direction of the strategic area north of Skoplje. Operation ROESLEIN cost the attackers almost a thousand casualties, but could not prevent a strong force from seizing a stretch of the highway north of Skoplje on 2 August; a hastily formed task force, with a reconnaissance battalion as its nucleus, managed to drive the Partisans off after heavy fighting. To the north, Operation FEUERWEHR inflicted more casualties on the Partisans, but could not prevent their movement into the upper valley of the Morava River.

On 12 August Operation RUEBEZAHL finally got underway, with the 1st Mountain Division and other German forces holding the major part of the advancing Partisan divisions and then driving them back across the Lim River. The results of the operation, though satisfactory in that the Partisans had been stopped from moving into Macedonia in force, were limited by the lack of a German parachute battalion, prevented by a shortage of gasoline from participating in the undertaking in its normal role. Also, the worsening situation with the Bulgarians and Romanians caused the German command to withdraw the 1st Mountain Division as soon as the operation had been completed, preventing exploitation of its success. Too, Partisan units that had managed to move to the east were now in position to threaten all road and rail transportation to the north and Belgrade.

On 20 August the Russians launched a drive deep into Romania, and on 24 August another of Germany's allies went the way of the Italians a year earlier. The German military headquarters in Bucharest was invested by Romanian troops, and tank units had to be rushed to its relief. A few days later, Romanian troops joined Soviet forces in a campaign to drive the Germans out of Romania. The Bulgarians, meanwhile, had begun to assemble their occupation units in Macedonia into a compact force in the area just west of their own national border.

On 8 September, Bulgaria was at war with Germany and the Bulgarian I Corps was already in contact with the Partisan forces that had managed to infiltrate east to the Moravia. Awaiting heavy Soviet and Bulgarian reinforcements from the Sofiya area, the I Corps held in place. Farther south, the V Corps was in defensive positions in east Skoplje, though units in and about the city itself put up a stubborn struggle against the 1st Mountain Division on its arrival in Treubruch. North of Skoplje, the 2d, 5th, and 17th divisions of the Partisan II Corps had been identified. Immediately engaging both Bulgarians and Partisans, the 1st Mountain Division cleared the main forces to the north and secured the city of Skoplje itself. However, the division lacked the strength to destroy the guerrilla and Bulgarian forces or to drive them from the area.

It is important to note, at this point, that the Germans had begun to use the Partisan and other guerrilla designations for the irregulars. Before this time, the usual reference in German reports had been to "bands." But from mid-1944, operations orders and the war diaries of the German units committed against the guerrillas began array the guerrilla forces as brigades, divisions, and corps, with numerical designation when known. In a conference on 21 September, Marrshal von Weichs expressed the view that the size, armament, organization, and operations of the Partisan units justified the Germans' considering them as an enemy on the same plane with the regular forces of the other nations with which the Reich was at war.

To keep the various small units and administration detachments over Yugoslavia intact while the fighting to secure the Skoplje area was in progress, Army Group F directed their concentration in central locations and the organization of an all-round defense. All female personnel wcre ordered evacuated, and plans drawn up to destroy all supplies that could not be moved. Outlying garrisons were stripped of combat units to build up the mobile force assembling under Second Panzer Army in the area south of Belgrade.

After an appeal by Prime Minister Neditch, the Serbian State Guard and security units were issued additional ammunition. Howit was obviously already too late to strengthen either the Serbian or the demoralized Croatian Ustascha. The Chetniks, facing complete annihilation at the hands of the Partisans, rendered some service in the capacity of security troops, but could not be depended upon not to attack small German detachments whenever the opportunity presented itself.

By late September Soviet forces were fighting north of Belgrade, in an encircling move to capture the city. The Second Panzer Army lacked the forces to implement German plans for an overpowering counterattack, and withdrew its weakened units into western Croatia. On the 27th of the month, Marshal von Weichs directed the impressment of all residents of Belgrade in the building of fortifications. However, threatened with encirclement, the command post of Army Group F had to be displaced to the north and west.

Belgrade fell to the Russians and the I Partisan Corps on 20 October. In the south, the rear guard of the German forces was approaching the Greek-Yugoslav frontier, leaving Greece in the hands of ELAS, EDES, and the British. Still in good order, the units of Army Groups E and F made their way to the northwest, keeping open secondary rail and road lines to evacuate the last of their forces from Macedonia, Albania, and Montenegro. Thousands of Chetniks, Serb auxiliaries, Croatian soldiers, and individuals who had assisted the occupation forces in one way or another joined the columns of withdrawing German troops.

The guerrilla movement at this point can be considered at an end. The resistance forces, with the assistance of the Allies and aided by the worsening German strategic situation, had finally been able to emerge as an organized force, be recognized as such by the Germans, and contribute materially to the liberation of their respective countries. In turn, these resistance forces had speeded the breaking of German power by tying down well over one-half million German troops and preventing their commitment on other fronts. In Yugoslavia, Tito was to become de-facto chief of state and crush his Chetnik opponents; in Albania, civil war was to ensue until Enver Hoxha and his communist faction could seize control of the country. With the military operations shifting to the north and west, the hinterlands of Albania and Yugoslavia and a large part of Greece became the scene of even more savage fighting as the communists made their ruthless bid for power.

CHAPTER 11

GEMSBOCK AND STEINADLER

TWO large-scale operations in mid-1944, one conducted in northern Greece and southern Albania, the other in northern Greece, may be considered as typical of Balkan antiguerrilla warfare. The terrain over which the operations were conducted was ideal for irregulars, with high and rugged mountains paralleling the roads vital to the extended supply lines of the occupation forces. The tactics used in both operations, surrounding the enemy forces and then narrowing and closing the circle, were the most effective means devised by the Germans for fighting guerrillas. Lastly, the guerrillas were fighting over terrain they knew well, an advantage balanced by the superior fire power of the Germans.

GEMSBOCK took place between 6 and 14 June, with the 1st Mountain and 297th Infantry Divisions, and the Division Group (Provisional Division) Steyrer, composed of a number of security battalions, participating. The 1st Mountain Division, as the strongest and most experienced, held the widest front, extending from Gramsh in the north, through Korca, to Vasilikon in the south. The 297th Infantry Division, in turn, held the line from a point west of Gramsh to Valona. On the south, Division Group Steyrer held the front from a point west of Vasilikon to the sea at Sarande. The XXII-Mountain Corps, directing the operation, had its command post at Vasilikon and the mission of destroying an estimated 9,000 ELAS and other communist irregulars in the rough square within the line Korca-Valona-Sarande-Vasilikon. The final assembly areas, to be occupied just before the attack, were situated as far as possible from the communist headquarters at Corovda, in order to prevent outlying guerrilla groups from escaping.

Despite detailed planning, the first phase of the operation was a risk in that each man had to cover a front of over 100 yards. It was of the utmost importance, therefore, that enemy intentions to effect a breakout be determined as soon as possible; this disadvantage would decrease as the circle was compressed. A shortage of fuel delayed the 297th Infantry Division in its movement to assembly areas, allowing the guerrillas time to collect their scattered units and devise a plan of defense. With the operation finally under way, heavy fighting developed on the front of the 1st Mountain Division, which succeeded in driving the guerrillas before it as the division moved westward. Probing for gaps in the German front, a number of small guerrilla groups slipped through the line formed by the 297th Infantry Division and fled to the north; the remainder of the guerrilla force moved southward, into the stronghold west of the road Vasilikon-Permet-Tepelene.

Reaching the road on the fourth day of the operation, the mountain division rested and regrouped to climb the almost vertical slopes west of Permet the following morning. With escape to the north and south now blocked off, the remaining guerrillas were compressed into the mountain area about Kuc and eliminated in another three days of hard fighting. The terrain, honeycombed with caves, had to be searched carefully and the guerrillas had to be killed or captured in hand-to-hand fighting.

GEMSBOCK cost the guerrillas over 2,500 dead and prisoners, and u large stock of arms; German casualties for the operation were 120 killed and 300 wounded.

Three weeks after the close of GEMSBOCK, the XXII Mountain Corps took the field in Operation STEINADLER, to destroy the guerrilla forces threatening the Korca-Yannina and Yannina-Trikkala roads. Attached to the corps for the operation were the 1st Mountain Division, a provisional division formed from elements of the Corps Group Salonika, and a number of security battalions. Estimates of the enemy strength were vague, but could probably be put at 6,000-8,000. Of considerable significance was the close liaison between these Greek guerrillas and the strong communist groups in Albania just across the frontier.

As a security measure, only the minimum number of commanders and staff officers were informed of the operational plan, while the troops were told they were assembling for a series of small-scale operations. Further steps to preserve the secrecy of the operation consisted of radio silence on the part of units moving into the area, small-scale troop movements in adjacent areas, and radio traffic from the light division below Arta indicating an attack farther south. The radio net operated by the guerrillas was monitored carefully to determine their reaction to these measures and to detect possible alerting of their units. Air reconnaissance was extended into Albania in order to allay guerrilla suspicions over unusual interest in the area.

Setting up its command post in the vicinity of Metsovan, the XXII Mountain Corps deployed the 1st Mountain Division along a line extending from that point to Yannina, Vasilikon, and Leskovic. Strongpoints and reinforced security units acting as a blocking force secured the road from Leskovic to the north and a junction with the Salonika Division Group near Korca. From a point east of Korca, the Salonika force was responsible for the line Bilisht-Kastoria-Neapoli- Grevena-Krania-Metsovan. Aware of their predicament as soon as the German troops had detrucked, the guerrillas evacuated Pendalofon and moved into the mountains. Air reconnaissance reported them still within the encirclement, however, and the troops continued their movement as planned. The first day ended with elements of the 1st Mountain Division held up by stiff resistance north of Metsovan. During the day, troops of the Salonika Division Group repulsed an attempt by a strong guerrilla force to break out at Grevena. On the second day, the Salonika Division Group was forced to halt and reorganize, having found it difficult to maintain cohesion over the rough terrain. The 1st Mountain Division, meanwhile, became heavily engaged at close quarters when it attempted to break through the resistance to its front. It was in this engagement that a battalion aid station, moved too far forward, was overrun by the guerrillas and eighty wounded were murdered and mutilated.

On its left, the 1st Mountain Division managed to forge ahead and on the third day enveloped the guerrilla pocket north of Metsovan, only to find a large part of the defending force had escaped to the northwest. Some 1,500 guerrillas were compressed in a ring about Pendalofon and destroyed in a systematic combing operation lasting two more days. STEINADLER cost the Greek guerrillas a total of 567 dead and 976 prisoners. In addition, 341 Italians and seven Britons were also captured. The booty taken included 10 tons of explosives, over three quarters of a million rounds of rifle and machine-gun ammunition, and 10,000 head of livestock, mostly sheep and goats. Despite these losses, the guerrilla forces began to regroup as soon as the German combat troops had left the area.

PART FOUR
RESULTS AND CONCLUSIONS

A compilation of casualties sustained by the combatants in the Balkans during the period of the occupation would not present a true picture of the enormous loss in personnel and materiel, or of real property. Actually, operations in that area during the period from April of 1941 to the end of hostilities were a series of struggles within the framework of a major war. A large number of casualties were suffered by both EDES and ELAS in their intermittent conflicts and in the civil war that followed the German withdrawal. The same was also true of Yugoslavia, where Chetniks and Partisans fought one another and the Germans at the same time. The Yugoslav casualties were further compounded by the Croat-Serb strife and the massacre of Serbs by the Ustascha, which occurred shortly after the establishment of the Croatian state. In Albania, the struggle between the nationalist and communist factions was no less bitter than the fight of both against the Italians and later the Germans.

In addition to the conflicts between nationalities within the same state and strife between political factions, there was also a determined attempt on the part of Serb Orthodox adherents of Mihailovitch to destroy the Mohammedan minority in Yugoslavia. The Germans added fuel to the flames of this fire by enlisting numerous Mohammedars in their forces and using them as occupation troops.

Finally, the occupation troops were composed of Italians, Bulgarians, and Hungarians, as well as Germans, and numerous foreign legionaries. While the Bulgarians were under German command, in large part, the situation was somewhat different with the Italians in that German units on coastal defense and in Italian-occupied areas were often under Italian command. Of the legionaries, some, such as the Russian Guard Corps, were integrated into the Wehrmacht, while others, for example the Serbian State Guard, were not. While the losses of the Russian Guard Corps would be counted among the German casualties, the personnel of the Serbian State Guard killed, wounded, and missing would not be, despite the fact they may have been fighting side by side.

Finally, German casualties from disease, chiefly typhoid, dysentery, and malaria, were unusually high, as were losses from direct physical exhaustion in the long marches and movements over rough terrain. The majority of the German personnel throughout the operations were of the older age groups and, except for the mountain units, had had little or no experience or conditioning for the type of warfare in which they had to engage.

On the basis of incomplete casualty figures, it can be said with some degree of accuracy that 1 out of 7 soldiers in German uniform, whether German or not, became a casualty by the close of Operations. At the time of the capitulation, thousands more fell into Yugoslav hands, when they did not manage to get clear of the Balkans to surrender to Allied forces in Italy or Austria.

All three occupied countries were impoverished by the peninsula-wide fighting and reprisals. Greece, a maritime country lost the bulk of the merchant fleet upon which it depended for its very existence. Yugoslavia, a grain-producing country that supplied food to much of southern Europe, could no longer even feed itself. Albania, the least developed of the three, lost a large part of the livestock upon which the national economy was based. In a 1-month period in mid-1944, a full quarter of all the locomotives in the Balkans were destroyed by Allied air attacks, a most serious loss in view of the inadequate road system and uneven distribution of food-producing areas. In Yugoslavia, the facilities of numerous mines were destroyed by sabotage, in the fighting to retake them, or demolished by the withdrawing occupation forces.

Perhaps the most significant results of the Occupation were in the political field. Two kingdoms fell, if Albania is considered, and replaced by communist dictatorships; Greece was prevented from sharing their fate only by the prompt intervention of strong British ground forces, supported by air and naval units. As was to be expected, the assumption of power by the communists was followed shortly by the elimination of all political opposition and the establishment of one-party states.

The successes achieved by the guerrillas against the Germans, Italians, and Bulgarians in the Balkans during World War II strengthened considerably the tradition of resistance to foreign occupation forces. Communist indoctrination of large segments of the population, with stress placed on clandestine methods and guerrilla tactics, also played its part in awakening this sentiment. Thus there is little doubt that a foreign invader today, whether from East or West, would be confronted with a formidable task of pacification following a successful campaign against the regular forces of the Balkan nations.

The experience of the German in their Balkan occupation also offers a number of lessons in the administration of conquered enemy countries and 1S a measure of what a future occupier might expect m that area. Before launching into a consideration of the sound as well as the injudicious aspects of the German occupation proper, however, it might be well to visualize the situation in which the Wehrmacht found itself in relation to its allies in Greece and Yugoslavia following the surrender of those two countries.

Regarded as the chief architect of their defeat by the Greeks, the Wehrmacht turned over the bulk of the occupation responsibility to the Italians in 1941. Already smarting under defeat in Africa at the hands of the British and having made a poor showing in their own Balkan campaigns, the Italians undertook no appreciable measures to prevent the growth of a guerrilla movement. The few Italian attempts at suppression, harsh and arbitrary, only kindled the resentment of the Greek population and placed a further onus on the Germans. Even more resented was the German invitation to the Bulgarians to annex Thrace, won at the cost of so many thousands of Greek lives in 1922-24 and still fresh in the minds of the bulk of the Greek population Yugoslavia, to appease Italian, Bulgarian, and Hungarian ambitions, was partitioned and temporarily ceased to exist as a sovereign state. Even worse, one large minority, the Croats, were granted their independence and then accepted into the ranks of the German satellites. Italian and Bulgarian reprisals for guerrilla activities, often inflicted on the innocent, alienated still more the bulk of the population, which also attributed the excess of the Croat Ustascha to the Germans as well as the Italians.

In their own zones of the occupied countries, the Germans exploited the economy for as much as it could bear, leaving the civilian population at a scant subsistence level and in many cases at a level so low that the relief agencies of neutral powers had to be called upon to prevent widespread starvation. This, the raising of native collaborationist forces to augment their own, and the obvious fact that there would be no relief so long as the Germans remained, placed the occupiers in a position that could only be held with increasing force as time passed. Shorn of allies by the defection of the Italians and Bulgarians, the Germans found themselves in possession of a rugged and largely mountain area seething with discontent, where even former collaborators were eager to join the winning side, well exemplified in the cases of EDES and a number of the Chetnik units.

In brief, this multinational suppression of the heterogeneous peoples of several national states was doomed to failure by the lack of central direction and the divergent aims of the Germans, Italians, and Bulgarians. Had one power alone administered the occupation and held out some hope of eventual relief to the conquered nations, better results might well have been achieved.

The system of parallel commands did not cease at the national level, in the German case, but extended down to the smallest units. While the Army, on the one side, was responsible to the Armed Forces High Command for the security of the Balkans, the SS was answerable to Himmler and his SS representatives except when engaged in field operations. Until the situation became critical and Marshal von Weichs was forced to assert his authority, SS units on occasion operated without Army control even in the field, and would cooperate in antiguerrilla operations only when it suited the individual commander and higher SS headquarters. Understandably, there was also considerable confusion and wasted effort in the operational and particularly in the clandestine intelligence field, with Wehrmacht and SS agencies trying to accomplish similar missions for their respective commands. This situation was further complicated by the activities of the German Foreign Office, which maintained its own version of a High Commissioner and was heavily staffed with personnel to accomplish political aims not always consonant with the directives given the military commanders. A single supreme authority representing the Reich, with clearly defined responsibilities, would have prevented much needless friction and waste of effort.

The German shortage of manpower reduced the forces made available for the Balkan occupation to the over-age anti the physically limited, with the exception of a few units such as the 1st Mountain Division. Other measures taken to alleviate the manpower shortage were the employment of native troops and enlistment of foreign legionnaires, chiefly Russians and Caucasus Mountains peoples. While the first group was capable of but limited service, the other was considered not completely reliable and requiring close supervision by German officers and noncommissioned officers. In either case, the conduct of operations was limited to their restricted capabilities and extended pursuit of routed guerrilla forces was generally unsatisfactory. Moreover, the equipment, particularly armored and motor vehicles, was below the general Wehrmacht standard and resulted in numerous breakdowns that might otherwise not have occurred. Motor parts alone kept vehicles deadlined for extended periods of time, until similar vehicles could be cannibalized and a reduced number of trucks, armored cars, and tanks could again be put into operating condition. Both personnel and vehicle situations were made unavoidable by the heavy demands of the active theaters of war, but it can be presumed that with personnel fit for full field service, properly equipped and mounted in more serviceable vehicles, fewer men would have been necessary to maintain order, and the results of operations would have been more satisfactory.

The German occupiers were very much aware of the importance of security measures required in their situation. Yet it is quite apparent that such measures were not adequate and seldom enforced. One feature of this laxity may be seen in the large numbers of local civilians hired to work in German troop areas and military installations. With only a most cursory security investigation, these Yugoslavs and Greeks had access to areas in which they could observe troop movements and preparations preceding operations, storage facilities for such sensitive items as gasoline and ammunition, and routine measures for defense. Since these civilians were paid by their own governments and presented no burden to the Germans, already overtaxed to provide personnel for operations, it is not too surprising that the occupiers took advantage of the opportunity to secure a large labor force. However, this convenience was more than offset by the compromise of almost every antiguerrilla operation of significance.

Commanders were reluctant to separate the troops from the civilian population entirely, both for morale reasons and in conformance with the German policy of exploiting the conquered countries even to the extent of having the troops buy up consumer goods for shipment home. This made unavoidable still more violations of security. In substance, the policy of the Germans toward the outwardly cooperative portion of the population was far more lenient than security demanded.

The German tendency to underestimate the guerrillas also played its part in the undermining of the occupation. At first, commanders felt the suppression of the guerrillas to be a function of the police. Later, when it became obvious the police could not restore order, the military commanders were forced to take the field. However, even after guerrilla activities had turned the Balkans into a theater of war, only intelligence reports carried the designations of guerrilla units; commanders still referred to these forces in their headquarters diaries as "bands." Not until 1944, when the guerrillas were threatening to drive him from the Balkans altogether, Field Marshal von Weichs acknowledge their strength and direct that reference be made to the guerrilla units as divisions, corps and other designations, rather than as "bands." Too, many of the demolitions and other technical operations of the guerrillas were ineffective and aroused the contempt of the Germans, but these were offset by their great number and the total amount of damage done.

A feature of significance but one over which the Germans could exercise little influence was the nature of the Balkan peoples themselves. Composed of hardy Greeks and Slavs, traditionally opposed to any occupier, they readily took up arms when it became apparent the conquerors intended to remain and to exploit their few resources; even the collaborationists often proved to be unreliable. Once started, the surge of the guerrilla-movement could not be stopped even by the wholesale slaughter of hostages.

It is unlikely that German commanders will ever face these occupation problems in the Balkans again. However, a review of the mistakes these commanders made would undoubtedly cause them to urge any future occupier to begin his administration with a clear-cut statement of policy, including a promise of eventual withdrawal of occupation troops and self-determination for the people; a unified military command and distinct delineation of responsibility in the political and military fields; the assignment of trained, well-equipped combat troops in adequate numbers to the area; the taking of prompt and effective though not excessively harsh measures to quell disorders; and an extensive propaganda campaign to explain the purpose of the occupation and the benefits to accrue to the population with the maintenance of law and order. Finally, they would most certainly recommend the troops be supplied from outside the country and restrained from excesses. With perseverance, the occupation forces might then be able to avoid the Balkan chaos of 1941-44.

REAR AREA SECURITY IN RUSSIA - THE SOVIET SECOND FRONT BEHIND THE GERMAN LINES

PREFACE

THIS pamphlet prepared by a committee of former German generals and general staff officers under the supervision of the Historical Division, EUCOM, in the early part of 1948. All contributors had extensive experience on the eastern front during the period 1941-45. The principal author, for example, was successively G4 of an infantry division and assistant G4 of a panzer army in Russia.

The reader is reminded that publications in the GERMAN REPORT SERIES were written by Germans from the German point of view. As in DA Pamphlet 20-230, Russian Combat Methods in World War II, and DA Pamphlet No. 20-231, Combat in Russian Forests and Swamps, the "Introduction" and "Conclusions" to this study present the views of the German author without interpretation by American personnel. Minor changes in form and in section titles have been made to secure greater clarity, and tactical examples have been rearranged to illustrate better the growth of the partisan front between 1942 and 1944. However, passages which reflect the author's prejudices and defects, whatever they may be, have not been changed and find the same expression in the following translation as they do in the original German.

This pamphlet supersedes MS No. T-19, "Rear Area Security in Russia," published by the Office of the Chief of Military History, Special Staff, U. S. Army, in July 1950.

SECTION I

INTRODUCTION

THIS study on the problems of rear area security is based on German experiences during the Russian campaign. Particularly striking examples have been selected which show most clearly the type of disturbances created by the Russians, the German countermeasures taken against them, and the lessons learned from experience. The same, similar, or different circumstances were encountered in other theaters of war. Accordingly, a variety of security measures became necessary and many new experiences were gathered. Yet, the fundamental questions remain the same everywhere.

Seen from the Russian point of view the problem might be stated as follows: "By what means or methods can I most effectively cut the lifeline of the enemy's fighting forces, either for a short time, or, if possible, for an extended period; where can I disrupt the line in such a manner that the effect will be felt at the front?" The answer is a definite combat method which has the typical characteristics of a blockade. It can be executed with relatively small forces and limited means; by allowing for the mobilization of the populace it represents a morale factor as well as an increase in fighting strength, while offering further advantages through the use of sabotage and espionage behind the enemy lines.

A country as vast as Russia, where many sparsely settled areas offer an abundance of shelter and concealment, naturally provides much greater possibilities for the use of this combat method than countries with different terrain. An additional factor is the strong natural inclination of the Slavs toward fighting from ambush and under cover of darkness.

From the German point of view, the problem might be approached in the following manner: "What active and passive measures of security must be employed in order to deprive such combat methods of their effectiveness or to reduce their effect to virtual insignificance?" Such considerations should not be confined to purely military aspects. In varying degree the politician, the public administrator, the military commander, and even the ordinary soldier have to deal with these questions. Uniformity in understanding and in meeting the problem, from the highest to the lowest echelon is a fundamental prerequisite for success. Furthermore, one should never be caught unawares by combat methods of that type. By careful advance study, not only of the country itself but also of the people, their customs, cares, and needs, as well as their hopes and desires, one must be prepared to meet such methods and even to anticipate new tactics on the basis of current experiences.

It should be emphasized at this point that whoever makes use of this combat method constantly gains new experience which will enable him to improve and intensify his actions. Different methods are developed from day to day, and some of them are likely to be fundamentally new. The tremendous technical advance of the last 10 years has placed entirely new and undreamed-of means of great effectiveness at the disposal of mankind. Even if one disregards the practical application of atomic energy, rocket weapons alone constitute a substantial element of destruction. Further possibilities may lie in the harnessing of nature's own functions. Just as science has recently succeeded in producing man-made rain, it is conceivable that a way might be found of causing a coating of ice to form on switch tower installations, turntables, and switches, so that railroad traffic may be temporarily paralyzed. At the height of battle such measures could be of decisive importance in hampering strategic troop movements, as well as transportation of fuel and ammunition. It would be profitable, therefore, to employ at an early stage the most capable experts in technology, physics, and chemistry who are able to apply, as well as to counteract, such modern methods of warfare. This is one field where no limit is set to man's imagination. At any rate, to be prepared means to save lives and to limit the range of those incalculable factors which must be expected in any war.

It is a fact supported by many examples in military history that events and conditions behind the front lines have often failed to receive sufficient attention. In all but a few cases this has worked to the disadvantage of the front. Combat forces, while they are in contact with the enemy, should never have to concern themselves with security problems of areas that lie behind them. That should always be the responsibility of higher echelons.

Rear area communications are comparable to the blood vessels of the human body. The most capable brain, the strongest arm, the most powerful heart can no longer fully perform its functions if the blood cannot follow its prescribed course through the vital arteries. It was with these ideas in mind that the following study was prepared.

During the Russian campaign, the most significant and instructive examples presented themselves in the area of Army Group Center.

From the wealth of material available for this study, primarily based on the personal recollections of the contributors who had taken part in the Russian campaign, only those examples were selected which had been duplicated by experiences on other sectors of the front. To that extent the present report may be considered generally applicable.

The areas of Army Group South (Ukraine) and Army Group North (Baltic States) were not favorable to partisan activities. Reasons for this are to be found in the well-known political conditions. Army Group Center, however, entered old Russian territory at the very outset of operations.

SECTION II
GERMAN PLANS AND PREPARATIONS

WHEN the first plans were laid for the campaign against Russia, the problem of security for all the necessary supply routes through the vast areas of the future theater of operations played a significant part. In the light of historical experience, a considerably greater enemy effort against the German supply lines was to be expected than in previous campaigns with their relatively short lines of communications, or in any of the areas already occupied. But the main point in all deliberations and the primary factor in all phases of military preparation was the vast expanse of Russian territory. Obviously, all supply routes would have to be considerably longer than ever before and thus more susceptible to incursions of all kinds. This was true not only for all roads, rail lines, and waterways, but also for all points at which supplies were to be stored. Anyone aware of these facts could virtually anticipate the location and number of probable danger points and the strength of the forces required to eliminate these security threats.

Deliberations over the type and extent of essential security measures led to the conclusion that, in this field also, a new approach had to be found. No longer was the main danger focussed on the same areas as in previous campaigns, for the operations zone of an army now appeared to be much less exposed than the areas farther to the rear. Areas in close proximity to the front are always the scene of strong concentrations of forces which have firm control over the local rail and road net and are in a position to keep the local population under close surveillance. In such areas it was, therefore, possible to maintain constant supervision and a high degree of security without employing a large force exclusively for that purpose. Any special security forces that were saved in this manner could be used to better advantage in other areas where the danger was greater, while those remaining in the combat zone could now be assigned to more specific tasks.

An entirely different situation prevailed in the rear areas where the vastness of the country, sparsely covered by German troops, presented a constant problem. Here, in view of the over-all manpower situation, only a limited number of widely dispersed occupation units could be employed. The constant lengthening of communication lines because of the rapid progress of operations produced an increasing need for security forces, a need that was even greater in the rear than in the vicinity of the front lines. These considerations determined all German plans for the protection of communication lines, a factor of vital importance to the outcome of the entire operation.

From the outset a distinction was made between active and passive security measures. For the purpose of active security, special units of various types and strength were created. At first they were organized in the form of separate battalions, and only in those instances where unusually extensive installations had to be protected were several battalions combined under the control of a security regiment headquarters. Most of their personnel was taken from older age groups and consisted largely of veterans of World War I or of men who had received a minimum of training in replacement units. They were led by older reserve officers or retired officers who had been recalled to active duty. These facts need to be emphasized for the better understanding of the difficulties which these units had to overcome later on in the performance of their tasks. Nevertheless, many of these security units gave an excellent account of themselves, particularly when the growing manpower shortage necessitated their employment as combat troops at the front.

They had a variety of weapons in altogether insufficient quantities. When the Replacement Army was no longer able to furnish an adequate supply of small arms, which were then more urgently needed at the front, the security units had to be equipped with captured Russian weapons. It is quite obvious that units outfitted in that manner and often inadequately acquainted with their new and unfamiliar weapons were extremely limited in their usefulness, except for areas where little or no trouble on the part of the populace was to be expected.

The unusual extent of all prospective operations in the East prompted the German High Command to lay plans for the establishment of a security organization that would be more or less independent of the armies operating in the forward areas. For this reason the area immediately to the rear of an army group operations zone was designated as an army group rear area (Rueckwaertiges Heeresgebiet). There, using his own forces, the army group rear area commander was to be responsible for all active security measures, for the pacification of enemy territory, and, consequently, for the protection of all lines of communication. Whereas in previous campaigns no more than weak security units had been organized and employed, the arrangement for the Russian campaign included ,the formation of entire security divisions, largely similar in composition and equipment to standard infantry divisions, but subject to certain variations depending on the availability of personnel and materiel. These units eventually proved capable of conducting an active defense against enemy forces appearing in army group rear areas. The areas assigned to individual security divisions varied in size from 5,000 to 10,000 square miles.

The security and pacification of occupied enemy territory behind the army group rear areas was to be the responsibility of the military occupation authorities, an arrangement that had fully proved itself during other campaigns. Their administrative agencies were to cover the occupied territory in a network of

Kommandanturen [Administrative area headquarters] of various levels, such as Oberfeldkommandanturen [divisional level], Feldkommandanturen [regimentaI level,] and Ortskommandanturen [company level]. Security forces of various strengths, as mentioned above, were to be assigned to these administrative units, depending on the size of the areas to be controlled. During the course of the Russian campaign, this organization made a substantial contribution toward the maintenance and security of German lines of communication from the homeland to the front.

Perhaps it should be emphasized at this point that to assure the security of future supply routes, active precautionary measures must be taken, even during the advance, to prevent the destruction of vulnerable objectives. This is especially true of the main supply carrier - the railroads.

On 22 June 1941, for instance, during the very first hour of the Russian campaign many road and railroad bridges were saved from destruction by the swift and surprising action of a few small combat patrols. Later these bridges were of invaluable importance to the entire German supply system in the East and in some instances actually provided the basis for further successful operations. During the course of the entire war, many objectives of vital importance to the transportation of supplies, such as bridges, underpasses, viaducts, railroad shops, and water supply installations were secured intact because of the energetic action of advance detachments. This was of particular significance in the case of railroad bridges which, if destroyed, would have required a long time to be restored to normal operation.

In the final analysis it was the master plan of the Chief of Supply and Administration which determined, more than anything else, the over-all structure of the security organization. Although recognized as a primary prerequisite, the immediate availability of the railroads as a carrier of supply could not be expected and, at first, was not taken into account. It was assumed that the roadbeds would be unusable because of demolitions, that the Russians would remove all their rolling stock, that the difference in gauge would necessitate the re-laying of tracks, and that partisan activity would be encountered. Therefore, all German plans for the movement of supplies were initially based on the use of the sparse road net that existed in Russian territory.

Armored spearheads were to be accompanied by heavy motor truck transportation units carrying supplies up to a distance of about 300 miles from the base. In this plan the supply of the more slowly advancing infantry divisions, which were equipped with horse-drawn vehicles, was also taken into consideration. The motor truck transportation units were to establish supply depots approximately 50-75 miles apart. These installations were to be set up in the immediate vicinity of large communities and preferably close to favorable railroad facilities. Particular emphasis was placed on the establishment of safe and adequate facilities for the storing of large quantities of supplies. As the combat elements continued to advance, a special security force was to be assigned to each of these supply depots to assure their undisturbed organization and improvement. The strength of these forces depended on the size of the installation, the area that had to be guarded, and the degree of danger from partisan activities. Generally, the plan called for a regimental headquarters with the usual number of security battalions in the case of a larger town, while a battalion headquarters with the corresponding number of smaller units was to be employed for the protection of smaller installations. As far as possible, front line troops were to be relieved of all such security assignments. As it turned out later, this policy could never be fully enforced.

The protection of these supply depots involved a variety of problems. Internal security consisted of guarding the supply dumps and adjacent buildings and facilities. Since these installations were to include warehouses for all classes of supply, as for instance rations, clothing, ammunition, fuel, medical and

Soviet partisans in Belarus 1943. The partisan on the left is carrying what appears to be a Soviet PPD-40 submachine gun. His companion is equipped with a Mosin rifle (with factory bayonet), plus German bayonet/dagger (on waistband) and two RGD-33 grenades.

veterinary equipment, as well as motor vehicles and spare parts, the need for security forces grew considerably as operations progressed. This circumstance had to be taken into account in all planning and especially in organizing security units. Furthermore, all installations necessary for the maintenance and operation of the supply depots, such as power plants, railroad stations, and airfields, as well as the billets of the security troops themselves, required additional protective measures. The mere fact that some of the larger supply installations might well assume the proportions of a medium-sized city may offer an indication as to the number of security troops that would become necessary.

The supply plan called for each newly installed supply depot to organize a forward echelon which was to move up behind the combat forces along the most suitable road. At these central supply depots, other smaller supply depots were to be organized and distributed laterally in both directions. In this manner the infantry divisions, regardless of their route of advance, could obtain their supplies without the necessity for long-distance hauls. A "block system" of successive guard posts was to be established to safeguard the flow of supply from one depot to the next.

In addition to the forces required for the above-mentioned tasks, security troops were to be furnished to the several armies to protect their base supply depots and installations and to relieve the combat forces as soon as possible of all security duties. Experience had taught that the actual combat elements were excessively burdened with such duties and thus often deprived of forces which were urgently needed at the front.

The initially established supply depots were to remain in operation until the Russian railroads could be converted to normal gauge and the supply bases advanced into the zone of operations. Then, as supply depots farther to the rear would be dissolved, their security forces could be made available for employment in forward installations. Another possibility for the release of security troops on an even larger scale would arise as soon as a previous zone of operations or an area under military control was taken over by a civilian administration. The police forces of this administration were then to assume the former duties of the security troops.

According to the original plan, the initial requirements of security forces were to be met by selecting combat units that had proved themselves during previous campaigns. Subsequent needs had to be covered by organizing new units. It was clear to all concerned that this plan would never produce a fully satisfactory result, partly because of the vastness of the prospective theater of operations and partly because of the limited replacement potential, which would certainly preclude the large-scale organization of units for purposes of security only. This view was later borne out in practice. To an ever increasing degree transportation and supply units of many types, and frequently even front line troops, had to be charged with the above-mentioned duties.

German plans for active security also called for an active air defense. Antiaircraft artillery units were to be provided for the protection of large or particularly important railroad stations, workshops, bridges, and similar installations. In each case the strength of these units depended on the availability of personnel and the importance of the installation. They were to be under the control of regional air force commanders.

Fuel trains and similar shipments, which at a later stage of the campaign became unusually valuable, were to be protected wherever possible by railroad antiaircraft batteries consisting of 20-mm. four-barreled guns mounted on flatcars. These units were under the command of the army group rail transportation officer.

Since it was quite obvious that both manpower and materiel for security purposes would be limited, special consideration was given to the problem of passive defense. Thorough training of all agencies arid forces concerned with the moving and handling of supply was recognized as a primary prerequisite for passive security measures. The combat troops themselves can contribute in many ways to the security and preservation of scarce and valuable supplies, and thus increase their own readiness for action as well as their combat efficiency. Combat and service troops alike received continuous instruction by appropriate directives and orders and were further trained by means of demonstrations and field exercises.

Of the many passive means of protection, the following may be mentioned: Over poor roads, through endangered areas, or at night long supply columns were to move quickly and without interruption; single vehicles were to avoid passing through partisan-infested areas; full use was to be made of the block system of security established along the roads by driving in convoy from block to block; and unloaded supplies were to be dispersed for protection against destruction from the air.

Particularly after 1943, as a result of experiences gathered during enemy air raids, unloaded supplies of all classes were generally placed underground. Only in this manner was it possible to preserve large quantities of supplies, which up to that time had been prize targets for the Russian air force. Protection for ammunition of all types was assured not only by means of dispersal but also by storage in tunnels and bunkers. In the case of fires caused by bombing attacks this method of storing had the obvious advantage that the spreading blaze caused considerably less damage to ammunition dumps than on previous occasions.

The precious motor fuels were stored in trenches protected by banks of earth on both sides. Drainage ditches were dug which, in the event of a large fire, would allow the fuel to flow off quickly and thus diminish the danger of an expanding blaze. The storing of rations required a greater expenditure of material and labor, especially in the case of valuable food supplies which had to be protected against spoilage due to moisture.

The passive air defense of railroad lines, buildings, and other railroad installations was carried out at the request of, and in close co-operation with, the regional transportation agencies. In army areas this was the responsibility of the local commanders, in army group rear areas that of the rear area commanders. Security forces of the type discussed in the earlier part of this study, particularly security divisions, were employed for this purpose. In areas where additional protection was required because of heavy partisan activities or the presence of important railroad lines, these security forces were at times supported by other German units that happened to be in the area, such as combat divisions which had been withdrawn from the front. As a last resort, the so-called emergency alert units were called upon which, though formed specifically for this purpose, were not too highly valued. In areas under the control of civilian occupation authorities, all security functions mentioned above were assigned to the regular police forces.

On many occasions, replacement transfer battalions and casual detachments en route had to be employed in the defense of endangered railroad lines. The trains themselves were protected by so-called transport security regiments. They were subordinate to the army group rail transportation officers and received their specific assignments from regional transportation headquarters. Troop transports and personnel on leave trains were responsible for their own security. For the protection of freight trains, cars were attached which offered observation and fields of fire over the entire length of the train.

Railroad lines and installations were protected by a system of block control points and by security patrols operating along the lines. In wooded areas both sides of the tracks were cleared to a width of 300 yards to prevent partisans from approaching without being discovered. Among the many protective measures developed during the course of the campaign the following might be mentioned at this point: One or more flatcars loaded with rocks were used in front of particularly important trains to provide protection against pressure and vibration-type mines. In some instances a whole train of empties was placed ahead of the train that was to be protected. Mobile construction units were distributed along the railroad lines. Amply equipped with construction materials and interconnected by a telephone circuit, they could be immediately directed to any point where the railroad had been damaged by enemy interference. At a later stage, when telephone poles became a favorite object of destruction for the partisans, demolition charges were inserted which would detonate if an attempt was made to cut or fell the poles. An item of civilian railroad equipment - a special mine-clearance device without crew - was placed in front of the trains to set off enemy mines in the roadbed by subjecting the tracks to continuous vibrations.

In the operation of the railroads, various protective measures were introduced. They included travel at low speed (at night not over 10 miles per hour); movement of several trains in convoy; rerouting of trains insofar as the lines permitted; and placing the locomotive in the center of the train in order to protect it from immediate destruction in case of mine explosions. Later on, when large numbers of Russian railroad personnel were employed, particular emphasis was placed on their closest surveillance.

Specific measures of passive air defense - a matter of paramount importance for railroad stations and junctions - comprised the transfer of all central switchboards from railroad stations to the outside, so as to create individual loop circuits. In the construction of new installations considerable intervals were maintained between buildings. As soon as they were occupied, all vital installations and all personnel quarters were immediately protected by every available means against the effect of bombs or fragments. Troops were frequently quartered in trains which were taken out onto open track at night.

In close cooperation with the supply agencies the unloading of all shipments was to be accomplished in the shortest possible time. As a standing operating procedure at night or during air raid alerts, all railroad stations were to be cleared of trains carrying ammunition and fuel. If supply trains could not be unloaded promptly, they were to be separated and their individual sections distributed as far as possible over all available spur tracks.

The aircraft warning service of units in the area was hooked up with the railway signal communication system, so that all traffic control agencies could be alerted in time and with maximum speed. If the wire lines were destroyed, these warnings were to be transmitted by radio.

As the above-mentioned plans and precautions indicate, the German Army High Command was by no means caught unawares by the strong partisan activities encountered during the Russian campaign. It was known for some time that the Russians were determined to use organized partisan warfare in the defense of their country and that they had used propaganda to spread the idea among their population. Their future military leaders in partisan warfare had been carefully trained in the use of this combat method. Just before the start of the campaign - according to information received in Germany - the Russian War Academy conducted war games in an area where certain locations were designated as so-called partisan centers.

Similarly, the Russian High Command had recognized at an early stage that, in contrast to the dense railroad and highway networks of the highly urbanized West with its ever-present possibilities for alternate routes, the very few serviceable supply routes through the vast expanse of the Russian area were of paramount strategic importance. Furthermore, in view of the great distances, the poor condition of the highways (which easily deteriorated under the influence of the weather), and the anticipated shortage of motor vehicles and fuel on the German side, the Russians realized that the main burden of supply would have to be carried by the railroads and that this would be equally true of all large-scale troop movements, furlough transportation, and evacuations. Clearly cognizant of this handicap, which would present itself in any military campaign against Russia, the enemy began early in the war to build up a "second front" behind the German lines.

SECTION III

THE FRONT BEHIND THE FRONT

1. Interference by Isolated Russian Units

During the first 6 months of the Russian campaign, the German supply system generally functioned without major interruptions. Either the enemy had failed to recover from the initial blow, or he was yet unable to muster the proper means for effective raids on German rear communications. Isolated attacks were made on German supply units, and at times entire divisions were cut off from their supply base for a short period. But actually this was always the work of organic Russian troop units or of groups of stragglers who, in their attempt to fight their way back to the east and rejoin their own forces, had to cross highways or side roads and on such occasions came into sudden and unexpected contact with German supply units. In these engagements, the supply troops were mostly at a disadvantage since they were hardly prepared to meet a fully armed opponent. At the very beginning of the Russian campaign the drivers of supply trucks, for instance, were inadequately equipped with small arms, and machine guns were lacking altogether.

In the fall of 1941, a heavy truck transportation company was proceeding along the Slutsk-Bobruysk road. The convoy consisted of 30 trucks with trailers and a crew of about 75 men. Because of excessive dust an interval of 50 yards was maintained between vehicles, which were moving at a speed of about 15 miles per hour.

When the leading truck rounded a curve, a large Russian cavalry force suddenly came into sight at a distance of about 1,200 yards - apparently in process of crossing the road from

126

A partisan commander teaching his fighters to use weapons, the Smolensk region, Russia.

south to north. At the same time the truck column drew fire from the front; what appeared to be an antitank shell went through the windshield of the leading vehicle and into the cargo without injuring anyone.

The truck stopped at once; its crew, with the exception of the driver, jumped off and took up positions about 25 yards ahead. An antitank gun was spotted in a ditch about 300 yards down the road. The company commander, who because of the breakdown of his own vehicle, had been riding on the leading truck, ordered his men to open fire on the Russian gun crew. Meanwhile the assistant drivers of the other vehicles had been brought up and placed in position. A motorcycle messenger was dispatched to notify the military commander of Slutsk and request assistance.

By now the enemy was also using machine guns and his volume of fire increased steadily. On the German side two machine guns and 30 rifles had been brought into action. Soon the first casualties were caused by the very accurate fire of the Russian antitank gun.

To save the vehicles, which were loaded with ammunition, the company commander ordered the drivers to take their trucks about 1 mile back on the same road and to wait out of sight with their engines running. Great skill was required to turn the 20-ton trailer trucks around on the narrow road. Screened by clouds of smoke billowing from the leading truck which had been set on fire, this maneuver succeeded. About an hour later the company commander received word that the order had been carried out.

After another hour and a half reinforcements came up from the rear and went into position. Finally, elements of a machine gun battalion arrived on the scene and its commander took charge of the fighting. The men of the truck company could now be withdrawn. Their losses amounted to one dead and seven wounded, with three ammunition trucks and trailers destroyed. Subsequent reconnaissance and interrogation of prisoners established that the truck company had run into elements of a 2,500-man Russian cavalry unit which had crossed the road on its way into the forest area south of Minsk.

The company had accomplished its general mission of protecting its cargo and of keeping it from falling into the enemy's hands. Had the convoy not been carrying ammunition, the outcome of a prolonged fire fight with an enemy of the described strength would have been extremely doubtful. Certainly the 30 rounds of ammunition which each man carried on his person would have proved inadequate. It was only because of the nature of the supplies loaded on the trucks that the enemy could be held at bay until reinforcements arrived.

At the time mentioned, the local inhabitants were generally cooperative everywhere. They welcomed the German forces as their liberators and desired nothing more fervently than to resume their normal, peaceful activities. This attitude was demonstrated in many ways. It was a common occurrence for mayors to request protection against scattered Russian soldiers who had formed bands in the deep forests and conducted raids against German troops and local inhabitants alike, primarily for the purpose of obtaining food, civilian clothing, and other necessities. Frequently, German supply units or delayed single vehicles had to bivouac in deep forests and passed the night without suffering any damage. On some occasions the local inhabitants actually warned German troops against bands operating in the vicinity and called their attention to specific danger spots.

2. German Attempts to Restore the Local Economy

The German combat forces, at least during the initial period of the campaign, made every effort to restore normal conditions in the areas they occupied and to gain the confidence of the local population.

In the summer of 1941, the eastward advance of a German infantry corps was halted temporarily by strong resistance near Rogachev in the area of Bobruysk. At the same time a supply bottleneck had developed which made it necessary to fall back on supplies that could be obtained front the surrounding territory. For the purpose of administration and local management the corps area, insofar as it was not affected by the fighting, was divided into subareas and placed under the control of the divisions. The area assigned to one particular division covered about 40 square miles and extended between the Bobruysk-Roslavl highway and the Berezina River.

Under the control of the division's supply and administration echelon the area was subdivided into districts similar to those of the former civilian administration. Each district was under the management of an officer or a civilian official of the division to whom a permanent interpreter was assigned. These officers and officials were relieved of all other duties and had to be present in their districts at all times. They were instructed to take up personal contact with the people, particularly with the older and more influential inhabitants, and to make every effort to gain their confidence.

Even in peacetime the area around Bobruysk had figured in the war plans of the Soviet High Command as a potential center of organized partisan resistance. As early as 1940 - as the Germans found out later - the Russian War Academy had made this area the scene of special partisan war games under the direction of General Kulik who was yet to play an important rode in actual partisan warfare. It was all the more remarkable that only 1 year later, because of their judicious handling of the population, the Germans were able to keep the inhabitants at peace and, moreover, to utilize the resources of the region for their own purposes.

When the area was first occupied, its peacetime economy appeared completely paralyzed. The bulk of its agricultural and industrial machinery had been either destroyed or removed by the Soviets. In keeping with the Russian mentality, all work in the cities was at a standstill and the fields lay fallow. Everybody seemed to be waiting for a direct order to start the wheels turning. As a first step in that direction all existing enterprises were seized and inventoried under the supervision of the district officers. Then all plants that were still adequately equipped received orders to resume operation immediately. In other cases attempts were made to replace damaged machines or missing materiel.

Russian mayors and collective farm managers were charged with the responsibility for getting the work in the fields under way, and soon the first harvests were brought in. Next, the grist mills, dairies, bakeries, and workshops of local craftsmen were put back into operation. Salvaged tractors, with fuel for them, were issued to the local civilian agencies. Egg collecting points, grain depots, and milk delivery stations were established. The marmalade factory at Bobruysk resumed operation under the direction of one of the division's disbursing officials who happened to have previous professional experience in this particular field. While the plant provided employment for many Russian laborers, both male and female, its products were welcomed by German troops and local inhabitants alike. All financial transactions were left entirely to the Russian civilian agencies, subject only to final supervision by German experts. No friction of any kind resulted from this procedure.

To assure the proper treatment of the Russian population, all German officers and noncommissioned officers appointed to these administrative posts were given a short orientation course by German experts on Russia. The redistribution of collective property was begun with the greatest caution, so as to cause the least possible disturbance to the general structure of the local economy. Collective workshops were abolished and henceforth every craftsman was permitted to practice his trade freely. For the repair and rehabilitation of factories and for their subsequent operation, skilled laborers were placed under the supervision of men with suitable background who were drawn from the German forces or even from the native population. The administration of state farms (Sovkhoz) was decentralized, and they were turned into local agricultural cooperatives.

Thus the division was soon able to cover at least part of its supply needs from local sources without actually robbing the country, while making a notable contribution toward the improvement of the overall supply situation. Within a short time a variety of articles was produced in the area under the division's administration. In addition to foodstuffs and similar items, the products included horseshoes, hardware made by local blacksmiths, and tow ropes for the horse-drawn units, especially for the divisional artillery. The local inhabitants were immediately reimbursed for all deliveries by certificates of value received, and the amounts were credited by the Russian local administration against their requirements of every-day commodities.

It was not without significance for the establishment of good will among the inhabitants of the area that one of the division's chaplains happened to be a native of Russia who had a good command of the language and was fully familiar with the Russian mentality. With the arrival of the German forces all churches had been reopened everywhere, and German troops and local inhabitants met in common worship. The news spread rapidly throughout the area; from afar Russian parents would bring their children to Bobruysk to have them baptized by the German minister in the newly opened church.

Once a feeling of mutual confidence had developed, the dance- and music-loving inhabitants arranged village festivals at harvest time which were regularly attended by German district officials and members of the security units.

Any arbitrary acts by German troops, such as the unwarranted slaughtering of cattle, plunder in any form, or the wanton destruction of property, were most severely punished. This served to protect the few possessions which the Soviet regime had left in the hands of private individuals and strengthened the confidence of the people in the fairness and justice of the German forces. For some time after August 1941, when it had to resume its advance toward the east, the division remained in touch with the area that had been under its control until increasing distance made all further contact impossible.

With the arrival of the occupation forces, which assumed control over the Bobruysk area following the departure of the German combat division, the picture changed from the very outset; the population was treated in a manner quite different from that to which it had been accustomed. Whereas previously certain regulations pertaining to freedom of movement in the area, curfew, etc., had been somewhat relaxed, they were now rigidly enforced. Every rule of common sense was suddenly replaced by strict adherence to the letter of the law. Such methods naturally had the effect of lessening the confidence of the people in the good will of the occupying forces. Particularly the well-meaning elements among the population, who had demonstrated their willingness to cooperate fully, were now sadly disappointed, whereas their opponents rejoiced and hastened to exploit the new situation for the benefit of the partisans and their counter-propaganda.

Eventually the new occupation forces proved incapable of taking effective measures against the partisans, who were now operating under the command of Marshal Kulik. The Germans gradually lost control over the entire area around Bobruysk, which became one of the most dangerous centers of partisan activities. German rear communications were continuously disrupted, while troop movements, railroad trains, and truck transports were harassed by persistent attacks.

The preceding example may serve as an illustration - even though on a limited scale - of the many advantages to be gained by the pacification of occupied territory, provided of course that forces are employed who are properly trained and adequately prepared for their task. This was not an isolated incident. Other German combat units were even more successful in enlisting the active cooperation of local administrative officials.

In the fall of 1941 a German division advancing toward Bryansk encountered heavy enemy resistance in the area of Pochep and had to assume the defensive on a broad front. As a result, the divisional supply point was located for some time at or near Mglin (20 miles northeast of Unecha). Here also, following the successful example of Bobruysk, a German military headquarters was established for the purpose of administrative supervision and area management, while the local Russian administration was reconstituted and staffed with new personnel.

In numerous meetings with the town council, arrangements were made for the resumption of work in local crafts and trades, as well as for the assurance of an adequate food supply. Soon the harvest was under way; then grist mills and distributing agencies resumed operation. It was even possible to reopen a print shop and a tannery which served the German forces, as well as the local inhabitants. With the aid of the Russian mayor, who was extremely active and willing to cooperate, a program was initiated for the repair of damaged housing and the construction of new dwellings. Offenses against the occupying forces were handled by German military courts with the cooperation and advice of local experts. In no instance was it necessary to inflict the death penalty or to take hostages.

In the town of Mglin and throughout the surrounding area peaceful conditions were soon established. Without disturbance the inhabitants continued to pursue their normal occupations. It was increasingly evident that after a short period, during which the activities of the German troops had been under careful scrutiny, the occupying forces had succeeded in gaining the confidence of the people. The same reaction was found even among the large Jewish population living both in the town and in the rural districts. During that entire time the front lines were no more than about Hi miles away. In all other respects the pacification of the area was accomplished in about the same manner as described in the preceding example.

When the division finally had to leave, it also tried to maintain contact with the region that had been under its control. But here again the same administrative blunders turned an initial success into failure. The occupation forces which took over proved incapable of protecting the population against the partisans, and quickly destroyed all confidence by their unreasonable treatment of local inhabitants. The police forces assigned to the area soon began to recruit forced labor and to persecute the Jewish elements of the population. Six months later this area also had developed into a hotbed of partisan activities through which supply transports were routed only in extreme emergencies.

3. The Rise of the Partisan Front

By late fall of 1941, occasional acts of sabotage by groups and individuals had become routine. The beginnings of a well-planned partisan organization that operated with a variety of technical and psychological means were clearly noticeable. A typical Russian institution based on national tradition, this organization grew steadily in size and importance throughout the entire war. (Ed.: See also DA Pamphlet 20-230, Russian Combat Methods In World War II, pp. 103 ff.)

There can be little doubt that by the winter of 1941-42 the basic pattern of the Soviet partisan organization had been established. To lay the groundwork in German-occupied territory, Russian agents under the guise of helpless civilians took advantage of the kindheartedness of the German soldier by passing through the lines and infiltrating into the army group rear areas. Other agents who had been left behind during the retreat of the Red Army gradually began their work. Many of them were women who felt that they could count on protection by the German soldiers.

Changes in the attitude of the population soon gave evidence of the incessant activity of thoroughly trained agents who made the best of apparent weaknesses of their German opponents. The people were told that the inevitable return of the Red Army would be a day of reckoning for all those who had collaborated with the occupying power. On the other hand, strong appeals were made to their national sentiment. "Shame and death to those who collaborate with the enemy! Save Mother Russia!" was a typical slogan. With great skill, the Russian propagandists exploited every mistake made by the occupying power in the treatment of the local population. Eventually these mistakes, more than anything else, served to undermine the initial confidence of the people in the Germans and in German propaganda.

Whereas the local inhabitants up to that time had been

friendly, trustful, and entirely willing to cooperate, their attitude changed greatly during that first winter. While they did not commit any overt acts, they clearly displayed more restraint in their relations with the German occupying forces. Many of them took great pains to avoid being seen during daytime in the company of German soldiers. It became more and more difficult to find men who were willing to accept local administrative posts. Here also the terror tactics employed by Soviet agents began to make themselves felt.

The next step was the formation of small bands which established their hideouts in the forests. They forced the inhabitants of the area to supply them with food and give support in other ways. At first their activity was confined to more or less coordinated raids on targets of opportunity. They attacked smaller German camps or supply depots, raided and plundered single vehicles on the road, blew up Russian industrial enterprises that worked for the German troops, and took with them any Russians who were working for the occupying power. Occasionally, they carried out demolitions of railroad lines which could often be repaired without major delay in operation. In some instances even German railway construction units working under insufficient protection were attacked and wiped out by partisan bands.

Early in 1942, in order to facilitate the movement of supply through difficult terrain or partisan infested areas, attempts were made by the German forces to restore some of the railroad lines that led into the corps sectors of the Second Panzer Army. Individual railway construction units were employed which had to provide their own security as they advanced along the tracks to make the necessary repairs.

In this manner, a railway construction company was assigned to the Bryansk - Dudorovsky sector, about 50 miles east of Bryansk. Strictly on its own the company worked for weeks on one particular section of the track. Eventually several days passed without any report being received from the unit. Investigations revealed that the entire company had been wiped out by partisans while it was working near Zhurinichi (15 miles east of Bryansk). All repairs on the section were immediately halted, and the line was of no further use since no additional forces could be spared to strengthen the security of the construction troops. The search for the partisans who had carried out the raid proved fruitless. Thereafter, to prevent the recurrence of such surprise attacks, railway construction units were no longer sent out alone unless they could maintain daily direct contact with nearby supply depots or combat troops.

By 1942 Russian partisan warfare against the German rear communications had entered a more advanced stage. A network of channels for transmitting orders, thoroughly planned in peacetime, reached from a central headquarters in unoccupied Russian territory up to the western border of Russia and, in some regions, even into Polish territory. Whereas prior to that time individual messengers, crossing the lines in the guise of harmless civilians, had sufficed to maintain communications and transmit orders, this task was now regularly performed by courier planes and even transport aircraft. These airplanes forwarded instructions to the partisan groups operating behind the German lines and supplied them with arms, ammunition, signal communications equipment, motor fuel, medical supplies and other necessities. They always carried full radio equipment to maintain contact with each other and their central headquarters.

That these flights were very numerous could be established by German ground and air observation; abandoned parachutes which were often found by German reconnaissance patrols offered very definite indications. Apparently the partisan planes operated only at night; they landed on well-concealed air strips deep in the swamps and forests or dropped their loads over temporary drop zones identified by light markers. Partisan headquarters, air strips, and drop zones were perfectly protected

137

by natural cover and impassable terrain obstacles. Although numerous radio messages emanating from partisan centers could be intercepted, it was impossible to establish the accurate location of their transmitters and to take effective countermeasures either on the ground or from the air.

In the fall of 1942, a German army operating southwest of Orel was ordered to assure the delivery of a certain quota of grain and potatoes from the local harvest. Agricultural control officers (landwirtschaftsfuehrer) were posted throughout the entire army area to supervise and direct the harvest operations carried out by the local inhabitants. Equipped only with small arms and scattered widely to include even the smallest villages in the area, these agricultural control posts could not be expected to offer effective resistance in the event of partisan raids. The harvest had no sooner been brought in when reports about increased partisan activities began to mount. Numerous partisan raids on harvest control points had the result of frustrating gradually the entire agricultural program until the German control organization was virtually driven out of all harvest areas.

Thus, in the absence of adequate security forces, which could not be spared anywhere else, the Germans gradually lost control over an area of great agricultural value. Local inhabitants reported that the partisans were continuously seizing and carrying off grain supplies. Other accounts indicated that Russian airplanes were landing every other night in the partisan-held forests around Bryansk, supposedly to pick up the grain seized by the partisans and to transport it to the east. These reports could actually be verified by German reconnaissance which observed landing lights in various places. But since these air strips were obviously located in areas held by strong partisan units, any interference from the outside was impossible.

In this manner the Russians succeeded in exploiting an enemy occupied area to the advantage of their own war effort, while the Germans, ostensibly the occupying power, were unable to take effective countermeasures. Thereafter, whenever German troop movements or antipartisan actions were carried out, they were also used as an opportunity for salvaging and removing local stores of all kinds.

In February 1942 a Russian plane shot down in the Orel sector was found to carry a recently completed moving picture film on the "Russian Counteroffensive Against the Invaders, Begun on 6 December 1941." The film was obviously intended to be shown in the rear areas in order to bolster the morale of the partisan groups and the local population. On their return flights from partisan areas such aircraft usually carried messages and reports, captured weapons, and wounded partisans. Occasionally, they even took along important German prisoners, as in the case of Brigadier General Max Ilgen who was captured in the German rear area and flown to Moscow during the same night.

Generally, the following may be said about the origin, type, and size of Russian bands operating behind the German lines: Organized partisan activity usually began with the formation of small, isolated bands of from 5 to 20 members who were hiding out somewhere in the woods. Even during the gradual buildup of the entire partisan organization, these basic units remained fairly independent. Their activity was initially confined to raids of opportunity conducted for no other purpose than to supply them with booty. What held them together was a certain spirit of adventure, probably a natural trait peculiar to many of their members. It did not take long until the over-all partisan organization extended also to bands of that type. They were fitted into a well co-ordinated plan and were employed chiefly to harass certain areas. In addition, larger groups were organized, some of which reached a membership of several hundred. Constituted along military lines and led and employed as military units, these bands differed only in their appearance from regular Russian combat troops. Most of their leaders were well-trained professional soldiers, some of them even general staff officers. They were brought in by parachute or glider or, wherever possible, were landed on partisan airfields. Most partisan groups were equipped with small arms and heavy weapons; a few even used artillery which the Germans had captured and then abandoned for lack of suitable transportation facilities after the encirclement battles of the first weeks of the war. On many occasions large bodies of Russian combat troops were separated from their main force and sought refuge in the dense forests. There they were organized into partisan groups and employed in operations against the German lines of communication.

In the spring of 1943 the Second Panzer Army, comprising about 35 divisions, was engaged in defensive operations in the Orel-Bryansk area. The main burden of supply was carried by the double-track railroad line Gomel-Unecha-Bryansk-Orel, which at the same time had to transport part of the supply for the adjoining Second Army in the Kursk area. A single-track railroad through Krichev-Surazh, which joined the main line at Unecha, was available for occasional use and provided some relief. Another single-track line from Smolensk through Roslavl to Bryansk served as an additional supply route. Motor transportation depended primarily on the main Smolensk-Roslavl-Bryansk highway. The road leading up from Gomel via Unecha, because of its exceedingly poor condition, was used only in emergencies. Moreover, it crossed some of the worst partisan areas and for that reason was bypassed whenever possible.

Strong partisan bands were located in the forests west of Lokot (south of Bryansk). They had been formed of Russian soldiers, cut off in the Vyazma-Bryansk encirclement battle, who now received their instructions from partisan headquarters somewhere in unoccupied Russian territory. Particularly during the Russian breakthrough into the Kursk area in the winter of

1942-43, they constituted a serious menace to the deep flank and the rear of the Second Panzer Army. In order to provide protection against these bands the Germans employed native units recruited in the area around Lokot. After the above-mentioned encirclement battle numerous Russian stragglers also were left in the forests around Kletnya and Akulichi west of Bryansk. Large sawmills located in that area were soon taken over by the partisans and, according to reports, some of the lumber was even transported to Moscow by air. The bands established in these forests conducted persistent raids on the road and railroad line leading to Roslavl. Thus the German communication lines into the so-called Orel salient were exposed to partisan attacks from all sides; the unpleasant consequences were soon to be felt in all supply operations of the Second Panzer Army.

The following security forces were available to the Second Panzer Army for defense against partisan bands and protection of German lines of communications: one security division to protect communication lines running north and southwest of Bryansk and to conduct antipartisan operations in the forests north and northwest of the city and in the area around Kletnya; several security battalions to guard the depots in the vicinity of Bryansk and to protect the road and railroad line to Orel, as well as the connecting roads in the area of Zhisdra; and native Russian formations to provide security around the town of Trubchevsk (south of Bryansk). These native security units had been formed for the primary purpose of protecting the local population against marauding bands of scattered Russian soldiers. From their hideouts in the forests, these bands made daily forage raids on the villages in the open country and subjected them to ruthless pillaging and plundering. The local inhabitants, therefore, had braved the dangerous woods to gather abandoned weapons, ammunition, and equipment for their own use against such attacks.

Partisans laying a charge on a railway line

All the security forces mentioned above were engaged day and night in antipartisan activities. They guarded the depots, bridges, and other vital installations. They furnished security detachments for the protection of trains that had to pass through endangered areas. On the roads they manned the control points established for security purposes and escorted the columns of supply trucks from one point to the next. In view of the large number of partisan bands and the vastness of the partisan-infested areas, it is not surprising that these security units fell far short of accomplishing all their tasks. According to reports by local inhabitants, it was in these forests that bands of White Russians had held out until 1926 or 1927 without ever being captured by the Soviet Government.

The partisans replenished their ranks in several ways. They brought in replacements from the unoccupied part of Russia; in their own areas they used the regular Russian conscription system to draft able-bodied individuals who were then trained in partisan units. Some of the bands acquired a high degree of mobility with the help of abandoned or captured German motor vehicles or by using sleighs and skis in the wintertime. Once a partisan band was known to operate in a certain area, one never knew just where or when it would strike next. That close liaison existed between the Russian leaders behind and in front of the German lines was clearly noticeable. Immediately before and during Russian offensives partisan bands were concentrated at strategic points, and their activities increased to the scale of major operations.

4. Attacks on Rail Communications

Throughout the Russian campaign the railroads remained the chief carrier of supply. German logisticians had hoped that the lines would be available and had constantly emphasized their vital importance to all operations in the East. But nobody had counted on so early an operation of the railroads as was actually possible in the course of the campaign. What this meant to all German movements was clearly recognized during the first muddy season in the fall of 1941, as well as during the winter that followed. Without the railroads all German supply operations would simply have come to a standstill. German motor vehicles, exposed to excessive wear and tear over roads in poor condition, were deteriorating rapidly, so that a considerable proportion of the motor tonnage was soon unavailable for the movement of supplies.

The enemy did not take long to recognize his advantage; the number of railroad demolitions through partisan action increased steadily. The methods employed varied with the purpose the enemy wanted to accomplish. Daily interruptions of traffic were caused by rail demolitions for which the Russians used various types of mines. Pressure- and vibration-type mines were placed in the track, to be detonated by the locomotives. To destroy particularly valuable supplies, such as gasoline in tank cars, the partisans used mines with pull-type fuses which were set off by remote control. Retreating Russian forces often buried mines with long-delay fuses, under the tracks where they might blow up as much as 3 months later. Mines with simple delay-type fuses were also employed to avoid hitting the previously mentioned protective cars ahead of the locomotive. In order to escape the mine detectors, nearly all of these mines were placed in wooden containers, and their construction was of the most primitive type; some of them consisted of no more than a small package of explosives with a safety fuze. Occasionally, even magnetic mines were used. They served as means of sabotage in workshops and on standing trains and were mostly equipped with delay-type fuses.

In the fall of 1943 four supply trains were destroyed simultaneously at the Osipovichi railroad station, and all traffic on that line had to be suspended for a long time. Investigations revealed that a magnetic mine had been attached, presumably by a native railroad worker, to one of the tank cars of a gasoline train. When the mine went off it set the car on fire, and the spreading blaze soon enveloped the entire train. An ammunition train standing nearby was ignited and blent sky high, setting fire in turn to an adjacent forage train. Finally, a fourth train loaded with "Tiger" tanks suffered the same fate and also burned out completely. The shortage of personnel as well as the lack of extra locomotives made it impossible to save even part of the trains by removing individual cars. Moreover, the explosion of the ammunition train had caused considerable damage to many of the switches, so that the line itself was no longer in operating condition.

Similar disruptions were caused when locomotives were fired upon with antitank rifles or bazookas. In addition, various acts of sabotage were committed by Russian railroad personnel who, for lack of German manpower, had to be employed in large numbers to keep the railroads in operation. About 110,000 Russian railroad men were used in the sector of Army Group Center alone.

At a later stage, demolitions were frequently combined with raids on disabled trains, which resulted in even greater losses of rolling stock and longer delays in the restoration of the lines. An excerpt from the monthly report of the Chief of Transportation, Army Group Center, covering the period from 1 to 31 August 1943, contained the following information:

"Despite the employment of special alert units for the protection of the railroad lines, partisan activity increased by 25 percent during August 1943 and reached a record of 1,392 incidents as compared with 1,114 for July. The daily average amounted to 45 demolitions. In 364 cases the rails were cut simultaneously in more than ten places. Individual demolition points amounted to 20,505, while 4,528 mines could be removed. During the night from 2 to 3 August the partisans began to put into effect a program of large-scale destruction. Numerous demolitions were carried out which caused a serious curtailment of all railroad traffic and a considerable loss of railroad materiel. Within two nights the six to seven thousand miles of track in the area were cut in 8,422 places, while another 2,478 mines were detected and removed prior to exploding. Several lines could not be put back into operation for a considerable time."

"Another major handicap in the operation of the railroads was the increasing number of sabotage acts, committed chiefly by native workers under partisan orders. These acts resulted chiefly in a severe shortage of locomotives. In many instances, the so-called eastern volunteer units (native formations) which were employed to protect the railroad lines made common cause with the partisans and took German weapons along with them. In one case, for instance, an entire Russian security detachment of 600 men went over to the partisans. On 17 August 1943 this force attacked the Krulevshchizna railroad station. Using the machine guns, mortars, and antitank guns which they had taken with them at the time of their desertion, the Russians caused considerable

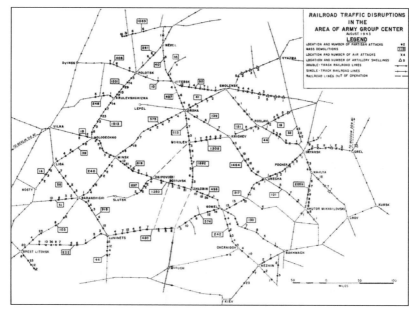

Railroad traffic disruptions in the area of Army Group Centre, August 1943

damage. German losses in that engagement amounted to 240 dead and 491 wounded. Altogether, partisan activities from 1 to 31 August 1943 resulted in damage to 266 locomotives and 1,373 railroad cars; about 160 miles of track were rendered unserviceable." (Map above.)

5. Railroad Demolitions

The operation of the railroads was often seriously impaired when their own signal communication lines were cut. This was usually done by sawing off or felling individual line poles. As a rule, such minor acts of sabotage were hardly the work of partisans but rather of otherwise harmless civilians who were acting under the pressure of Soviet agents.

With time the partisans developed a definite system in the disruption of railroad traffic. In support of major operations, for example, they were no longer satisfied with destroying the lines at certain points but carried out mass demolitions with the effect of disabling long sections of the track. Partisan operations on the ground were often combined with attacks from the air directed

146

primarily against railroad stations, rail junctions, bridges, and particularly important railroad lines. Such actions, as previously mentioned, were carefully co-ordinated and usually indicated that the enemy intended to launch an attack against the German lines.

Until the fall of 1942 Russian air activity against German supply lines was confined to isolated attacks which did not appear to follow any definite pattern. There were occasional bombings of railroad stations, supply dumps, or roads, but these raids did not cause major disruptions or traffic jams. The situation remained virtually the same during the winter of 1942-43. But a radical change came with the spring of 1943 when the German forces began their strategic concentration for an offensive south of Orel (Operation Zitadelle) .

At first the main railheads at Orel and Bryansk were blasted day after day by the Russian air force. The loss of supplies and railroad materiel was felt immediately, since the lines were now not only serving the Second Panzer Army but also bringing up supplies in preparation for Operation Zitadelle. At Orel a supply train loaded with one million rations received a direct hit and went up in flames. As the fire spread, it destroyed an army ration dump which had not yet been dispersed and placed into underground shelters.

At the eastern edge of Bryansk, bombs were dropped on an ammunition dump which resulted in the loss of about 1,200 tons of ammunition. The Bryansk railroad station was hit repeatedly at the peak of its night traffic. In contrast to the usual procedure the station had to be kept in operation at night because of the heavy load carried by the feeder lines. On one of these occasions a train loaded with ammunition for the Second Panzer Army was blown up, and the fire spread to another train carrying the equipment of a division in transit. Consequently, the entire reserve supply of arms and equipage of that division was destroyed. As another ammunition train was leaving the station;

the last few cars were hit by bombs and the train was set on fire.

As a countermeasure, all army supply dumps in the area were immediately separated into smaller dumps. 'I'his could only be accomplished by using all temporarily available motor transportation, chiefly, corps and division vehicles, with the added disadvantage that now even more security forces were required than before. Moreover, the new dumps were no longer close to good railroad facilities. This, in turn, tied down an excessive number of vehicles and caused the consumption of more gasoline. Wherever possible, supply trains were broken up before reaching tile unloading stations and rerouted by individual carloads to those corps which had their own railroad facilities. The railroad stations were completely cleared of all cars by nightfall. Another countermeasure was the unloading of supply trains somewhere along the line, just prior to reaching the last damaged section of the track. At such points the supplies were transferred directly to organic army vehicles or even to trucks of the front-line units proper. But this again was a measure which required additional personnel, tied up a large number of trucks, and caused a substantial increase in the consumption of gasoline. Therefore, it was soon necessary to reroute supply shipments over the Roslavl-Bryansk line, which became the next major target for Russian air attacks.

The Seshchinskaya railroad station, 55 miles northwest of Bryansk, was completely destroyed by heavy, successive bombing raids. In that area the highway ran close to the railroad line, and the temporary destruction of both made it extremely difficult to bring up the men and materiel required for repairs. For some time supply trains were taken only as far as Roslavl, and from there all supplies had to be carried forward by army group trucks. All available repair units were now placed along the main railroad line in order to restore it as quickly as possible to full operating capacity. They succeeded for short periods of time, and soon individual supply trains could be pushed through as far as Bryansk or at least to a point outside of Pochep where the supplies could be transferred to motor-trucks.

When the enemy realized that he could not bring about the complete isolation of the Orel salient by air attacks alone, he tried to disrupt the German lines by ground tactics. In a series of demolitions, the partisans cut the main railroad line as far back as Gomel. In this situation again the close cooperation between the partisans behind and the enemy forces in front of the German lines, with all its detrimental effects upon the German supply situation, became clearly noticeable. As a last resort, some of the trains were now diverted over the single-track Krichev-Unecha line. In the absence of any reserve forces, there was no way of strengthening the security of roads or railroad lines. But in spite of all obstacles and difficulties, the Germans managed time and again to get a lone supply train through to Bryansk.

Meanwhile, the offensive plans of the Russian forces facing the front and the flanks of the German salient had become apparent. On the German side the need for supplies became even greater than before. Corps and divisions had to use every imaginable expedient in replenishing their dwindling supply from army dumps.

In March 1943, the main supply line into the Orel salient was completely interrupted for some time. The break occurred about 15 miles southwest of Bryansk where a double-span railroad bridge crossed the Desna river. The paramount importance of this bridge had been impressed upon the commander of the rear area, and he had been repeatedly warned that the structure was to be protected and kept intact at all costs. The commander had therefore assigned a security platoon with antitank weapons to the task of guarding the bridge. One of the German reliefs which failed to take the proper precautions and was observed by the enemy from the neighboring woods, fell victim to a partisan night attack. The leader of the covering force had neglected to assign his men before nightfall to their individual defensive positions. At the crack of dawn the partisans first made a feint assault from the west. Once they had succeeded in distracting the attention of the security unit, a group of 200 to 300 men attacked the bridge from the east; the guards were overrun and the bridge blown up. The main line was now blocked to all traffic.

All available railway engineer and maintenance forces were immediately put to work to deal with this emergency. They constructed crib piers of railroad ties which had to rise to a height of 60 feet. It took 5 days before the improvised structure was usable for single freight cars, and these had to be moved across by hand. After little more than a week the bridge was capable of supporting entire trains without their locomotives. Each train had to be pushed on to the bridge from one side and pulled off from the other.

During the same night in which the bridge was destroyed, other partisan forces disabled the relief line running from Krichev to Unecha by cutting it in 90 places over a total length of about 60 miles. As a result, both lines were out of operation at the same time.

During the night of 19-20 June 1944 the partisans carried out a major operation in the area of Army Group Center. This was 1 day prior to the Russian general offensive which eventually led to the collapse of the German Army Group. Altogether, the partisans attempted 15,000 demolitions on the railroad lines running through the area and were successful in 10,500 cases, all in the course of 1 night. Their main effort was directed against the supply lines that served the Third Panzer Army, the same German unit which was to bear the brunt of the first heavy attack by the Red Army on the following day.

As an immediate result, all double-track lines were blocked for a period of 24 hours, while the operation of single-track lines was interrupted for over 48 hours. This was another example that demonstrated the excellent coordination between the Russian combat forces and partisan headquarters behind the German lines. Obviously, the sudden collapse of its entire rail transportation system had disastrous effects upon the operations of an army group engaged in a desperate struggle at the front. It was too late to apply effective countermeasures, and only a few temporary expedients could be found to relieve the situation.

6. Disruptions of Highway Traffic

The undue burden on the railroad net, coupled with a widespread lack of efficient railroad lines, forced dependence on highway transportation for a substantial part of all supply shipments. As a result, the roads soon became favorite targets of partisan raids. This was especially true for stretches leading through dense and extensive forests, where the partisans found perfect concealment and could not be pursued by German troops. The tactics employed in these raids followed generally the same pattern: A German motor convoy traveling through a dense forest would suddenly run into a log barrier constructed at a blind spot on the road and, while coming to a halt or trying to turn, would be exposed to devastating enemy fire from all sides. If any vehicle managed to escape to the rear, it was only to be caught and destroyed in another road block set up by the partisans in the meantime.

Cutting of telephone lines was another means of paralyzing road traffic. It always called for a time-consuming and painstaking effort on the part of the line crews who had to find and repair the breaks.

The partisans frequently laid mines on the roads. Without causing any serious damage this had the effect, at least, of blocking traffic for short periods of time. Virtually all of these mines were no more than wooden boxes of primitive construction, filled with various kinds of explosives and equipped with a simple pressure-type fuze. Because of their nonmetallic containers they could not be picked up by German mine detectors. Actually these mines had no greater effect than to damage or destroy the wheel which had run over them. Seldom did they cause any casualties among the drivers.

In the early stages of the campaign single vehicles were sometimes attacked by well-concealed Russian snipers. Even later, during their first fire raids on German convoys, the partisans usually remained out of sight. As their strength increased, they began to carry out regular attacks on highway traffic, using the same tactics as in their raids on railroad trains. The partisans would open surprise fire on a German motor convoy and then go over to a regular infantry attack which usually ended with the destruction of the vehicles, capture of the crews, and seizure of the supplies. In many cases the bodies of German soldiers who had belonged to the raided convoy were found later with all signs of having been brutally murdered by the partisans.

Bitter experience taught the Germans that the most dangerous roads were those that ran through impenetrable and often swampy forests, which by European standards were of gigantic size. It was practically impossible to advance into these woods for more than a mile or two, since anyone not familiar with the terrain would be left without a path and unable to find his bearings. Therefore, the Germans established a system of security strong points along all roads leading through partisan-infested areas. Single trucks were no longer permitted to pass through the forests. Depending on the degree of danger in each case, motor convoys of ten to thirty trucks with adequate crews and sufficient protection were formed and escorted through the partisan-infested woods from one control point to the next.

At the beginning of tile Russian campaign the crews of German supply trucks had small arms, but no machine guns. Later on, after some truck convoys had been helplessly exposed to surprise fire and partisan raids, they were issued machine guns which were mounted on the platform of 1/2 to 1-ton trucks. At a still later stage of the campaign the trucks were lightly reinforced with armor plates. Shortage of personnel, however, precluded the use of special machine gun crews and placed an additional burden on the supply troops. On every-trip the relief driver had to sit behind the machine gun, ready to fire, while the rest of the convoy personnel was constantly on the alert against surprise attacks. Soldiers returning from furlough were sometimes collected at security strong points along the roads and employed as escort personnel for supply convoys moving up to the front.

7. Attacks on Supply Depots

Now and then the partisans raided German supply dumps in army rear areas. But compared to other partisan incursions, such raids were quite infrequent, perhaps because these dumps and distributing points were usually located close to the front and therefore more strongly protected against surprise attacks.

The personnel in every supply installation, in addition to their regular work, were charged with interior guard duty and the protection against enemy attacks on the ground and from the air. A perimeter defense plan was drawn up for each installation. In case of attack prepared positions indicated in this outline were to be occupied and held by all personnel present at the installation. In most instances, however, the projected field fortifications could not be completed because of the pressure of time. A complex communications network consisting of radio, telephone, motorcycle messengers, and runners assured the rapid transmission of orders, reports, and calls for immediate assistance.

Russian air attacks on German supply installations showed a marked increase in 1942 and 1943. During the first winter of the campaign Russian air activity had been confined to isolated attacks by so-called "sewing machines" - obsolete aircraft with noisy engines - which dropped single, small-sized bombs and did little damage. But soon thereafter the Russians began to concentrate their air attacks on German supply lines on an ever increasing scale. Soviet air reconnaissance seemed to pay special attention to locating German supply installations; in contrast to the preceding period, even supply dumps close to the front were now subjected to frequent raids.

Wherever the supply troops used adequate precautions, these raids caused relatively little destruction. Major damage was prevented in most instances by maintaining proper safety intervals between stacks or burying supplies in the ground, as well as by the unhesitating commitment of all available personnel in case of emergency.

There was no evidence that the Russian civilians living in the immediate vicinity of these German supply dumps ever used their knowledge to pass information to the enemy, promote acts of sabotage, or facilitate partisan raids. While few of these advance supply installations were ever attacked by the partisans, it was established that in one particular area partisan convoys led by German-speaking individuals in German uniforms called for provisions, and by the presentation of the regular requisition forms they managed to obtain German supplies. This was made possible by the fact that the German forces were using almost exclusively Russian personnel for their so-called panje-convoys (columns of native horse carts), with only a few Germans to supervise them. Thus it was relatively easy for the partisans to organize the same type of convoys without attracting undue attention and to disappear again as soon as their mission was accomplished.

German supply traffic on Russian inland waterways was seldom subjected to enemy interference; no instance is known in which the Russians mined their rivers. Wherever possible, river craft used for supply and transportation by the German forces were provided with makeshift armor and equipped with light guns.

CONCLUSIONS

A. From the wealth of practical experience gained during the Russian campaign and particularly from the foregoing examples a number of important lessons can be derived.

1. The employment of peaceful means clearly offers the best assurance for military security in an occupied area. Failing that solution the only alternative lies in an all-out program of active defense.

2. In the selection and organization of security forces, despite the usual difficulties, the main emphasis must be placed on the high quality of personnel and equipment. No partisan-infested area can be cleared and rendered permanently safe by a force composed of old men who are equipped with foreign weapons and a few rounds of ammunition. If such security units fail to accomplish their mission, they are likely to become the laughing-stock of an inherently antagonistic population and their ineffective operations will have the result of strengthening the resistance of the enemy.

3. Anyone charged with responsibility for planning and conducting military operations must take into account the size, danger, and proper significance of the front behind the front. Any disruption of German rear communications anywhere in the vast expanse of occupied Russian territory was sure to have immediate effects which could be felt by virtually every German headquarters, indeed by every single unit. No similar experience had been made in any of the previous campaigns, with the possible exception of the Balkan operations. The full implications of this new problem became particularly obvious whenever the German armies in Russia were confronted with the perfect teamwork

between the enemy behind their lines and the Russian forces in front. What happened in the rear area frequently served as a clue to the enemy's intentions at the front. It might be mentioned that German troops harbored no illusions about the nature of this added theater of operations. It did not take long until word was passed among the divisions on the line that the fighting against the partisans for the protection of rear communications was often more severe and resulted in larger numbers of casualties than actual combat at the front. Many a division brought to the rear for rehabilitation and there, as a sideline so to speak, employed in antipartisan operations, requested after a short time to be relieved of such duties and permitted to return to the front. This reaction alone should well support the contention that the front-behind-the front is a theater of operations in its own right. No longer is it appropriate to treat this zone as a stepchild or to regard it merely as the zone of communications in the traditional sense.

4. Any commander who is determined to conduct an active defense against partisan bands must of necessity accept the idea of committing regular combat forces in occasional mopping-up operations of partisan-infested areas. German experience during the Russian campaign clearly demonstrated that a passive defense based on scattered security strong points is not sufficient, no matter how well such a defense may be organized.

5. The greatest promise of success lies in carrying the fight against partisans beyond the immediate vicinity of threatened supply lines and right up to the enemy's strongholds and rallying points. Careful reconnaissance is a paramount requirement for such operations. Without adequate knowledge of the terrain any expedition into a partisan-infested area can be no more than a plunge in the dark and will only lead to excessive losses in men and equipment.

German paratroopers interrogating a Soviet partisan, summer 1942

Another prerequisite is the current maintenance of accurate maps which cover the pockets of resistance and the assembly areas of partisan groups. Data for these maps can be obtained from local sources if the occupying troops are able to gain the confidence of the indigenous population.

6. Constant patrolling activity must be maintained not only on the main highways but also along the side roads. Occupied areas are to be kept under close surveillance at all times through a regular network of interlocking patrol posts. But even such patrols will only serve their purpose if at least some of their personnel are acquainted with the country and able to obtain information and reports from the local inhabitants. Therefore the careful selection and judicious employment of men who are familiar with the terrain, the language of the people, and the enemy's military tactics are among the principal prerequisites for the success of an active defense.

7. Commanders of village strong points or of local security units are to be granted complete authority for local

antipartisan operations. This will enable them to take aggressive and successful measures immediately at the appearance of partisan bands, and obviate any lengthy and time-consuming inquiries or requests to higher headquarters. Small motorized forces must be available for the rapid pursuit of the enemy. Partisans operate at great speed; they appear on the scene, complete their mission, and withdraw again to their hideouts. Once they have disappeared into the woods, it is practically impossible to pick up their tracks.

8. Of equal importance is the constant use of aircraft for the surveillance of areas that are suspected or known to be infested by partisans. This is especially true of large forest regions. Wherever local terrain conditions render any ground reconnaissance impossible, it is only from the air that a rough estimate can be obtained of the whereabouts and activities of partisan forces.

9. It is clear, nevertheless, that there must be another solution to the entire problem of rear area security. In modern warfare even an active defense based on the combined efforts of combat troops and security forces cannot assure the complete elimination of partisan activities. In the area of Army Group Center, for instance, there were 80,000 to 100,000 partisans, who tied down a security force conservatively estimated at 100,000 men. The use of front-line divisions in mopping-up operations on a large scale - such as the combing of the Bryansk forest in the spring of 1943 - had no more than a temporary effect; in no instance did the result of such operations justify their cost.

10. The only all-inclusive solution to the problem of rear area security seems to lie in the actual pacification of occupied enemy territory. In every country under military occupation there are people in all walks of life whose most ardent desire is the return to peace and normalcy, not to speak of those among them who for personal reasons are willing to support

the policies of the occupying power. Cultivating their friendship, assuring them of one's peaceful intentions, and restoring the safety of their homes, their work, and their subsistence are the best guarantees for real security in the rear of the fighting troops.

11. News of good treatment travels just as fast as reports of bad treatment, and most people will decide quickly and intelligently what kind of treatment they prefer. Generally speaking, the civilian population in Russia was quite willing to cooperate. Moreover, the villagers themselves were ready to defend not only their homes but also their places of work against native plunderers, Red Army stragglers, and raiding partisans. The reopening of places of worship and the revival of long-neglected church services contributed greatly toward the establishment of good will.

12. Many other examples pointed to the wisdom of a policy of pacification. Although friendly and cooperative in the beginning, the inhabitants of some areas were soon driven into the arms of the partisans by improper treatment or unwise occupation policies. German military commanders or their troops were always the least to be blamed for such developments. But whenever an area was turned over to a German civilian administration, it did not take long until the attitude of the population changed from collaboration to hostility.

B. What then are the methods by which the indigenous population can be won over ? What must be done to establish and maintain the security of rear areas ?

1. The first and foremost prerequisite is the full confidence of the population in the good faith, as well as in the military capabilities of the troops fighting at the front or occupying the rear areas. Such confidence can be created by a sound, straightforward, and factual propaganda prepared and disseminated by individuals who familiar with the Russian

language, the population, and local living conditions. Extraneous ideas are to be avoided; whatever the people are told must be expressed in their own everyday language, on their own intellectual level, and concerned with their own immediate problems.

2. A thorough knowledge of Bolshevist doctrines and methods is indispensable, especially of those aspects which in the past have imposed hardships and suffering on the population. While being reminded of their unpleasant experiences, the people must be shown the road to freedom from Bolshevist oppression and communist ideology.

3. The Russian is a great believer in official papers. He is happiest when he has an official document, a stamped identification card, or an official pass in his hands. This propensity is to be cultivated, since it offers a fine medium of propaganda.

4. Typical Soviet propaganda methods, such as placards, bulletin boards, and oversize posters, should not be copied. If the Russian has little faith in Bolshevist propaganda, he will put even less in its imitation. He can be strongly influenced by pictures and statistical charts, provided that they are used to present clear and simple facts. At the same time an appeal to his emotions should be made in the wording and visual presentation of the propaganda material.

5. The Russian is not interested in pin-up girls. He wants to be told about western machinery, industrial operation, and farming; about the methods and profitableness of western private enterprise. He has toiled long enough for State and Party. Now he would like to know in what way and to what extent he may work for himself. In this respect he is looking for the help of the occupying power.

6. Propaganda, to be effective in Russia, must not operate with far distant goals, since Bolshevism presented the Soviet people with too many long-range promises in its Four Year

Plans. The individual Russian wants to know:
- What will I get from the next harvest?
- May my children go to school?
- May they freely choose any vocation ?

7. Russian youth want to have the right of choosing and freely practicing a profession. The Russian girl is not too domestically inclined; she is primarily interested in achieving an equal standing with men in all occupations.

8. Propaganda in occupied enemy territory must advocate measures which are practicable even in wartime and develop programs which can be put into operation prior to the termination of hostilities. The immediate aim must always be in the foreground; no more than a general outline should be given of the long-range goal.

9. The foremost propaganda agent is the individual member of the occupying forces, the mall who is able to talk and associate with the Russians everywhere and to tell them what they want to know. At the same time he must have full authority to issue local regulations since it is well known that the Russian waits for directives, orders, and permits, rather than doing anything on his own. Convinced that it will harm him in the end, he avoids independent action wherever possible. But whatever he is ordered to do, he does willingly and wholeheartedly. This is an outgrowth of Russia's historical evolution under both czarist and communist rule, as well as an inherent national characteristic.

10. Speeches at public rallies or in meetings of municipal councils are an effective medium of propaganda. By far the best results are achieved wherever propaganda can be disseminated by word of mouth.

11. It goes without saying that the actions of the occupying forces must be in strict accordance with their propaganda. The start or resumption of work by the civilian population is to be ordered, but no forced labor must be permitted. Civilian

food requirements are to be assured at a minimum subsistence level. Arbitrary actions by either the occupying power or the local administrative agencies are to be avoided under any circumstances. The resumption of work in native crafts and trades is to be given all possible aid and encouragement. Spiritual activities and religious freedom are to be restored by reopening the churches and protecting public worship.

12. Prisoners of war are to be well treated and used for productive work only. Wherever their presence is not needed and they are not likely to jeopardize the security of the occupying forces, they are to be released as soon as possible. Experience has shown that the early release of prisoners of war contributes greatly to the pacification of occupied territory.

13. Although as a general rule the free movement of civilians must be confined to their local communities, exceptions should be made to permit securing of food, attendance at public worship, and necessary travel in the event of illness.

14. The importance of work for everyone, with the assurance of adequate pay and subsistence, cannot be overemphasized. Unemployed and discontented masses of people, lacking the bare necessities and perhaps exposed to arbitrary acts at the hands of the occupying troops, represent an enormous danger to rear areas and communication lines. This is all the more true in the vast territory of Russia, where such dissatisfied elements are offered innumerable opportunities to disappear in forests and swamps, in the wilderness, and on river islands. Here nature provides fertile soil for the rapid growth of partisan bands.

SMALL UNIT ACTIONS DURING THE GERMAN CAMPAIGN IN RUSSIA: ANTIPARTISAN WARFARE

I. General

Guerrilla warfare is as old as time itself. During more recent times this type of operation has assumed an ever greater importance in military and political planning. That the study of partisan and antipartisan combat methods is an absolutely essential element of any up-to-date military training program is obvious. Based on practical German experience in Russia, the following examples are certain to stimulate interest in this subject.

Partisan operations do not conform to any hard and fast tactical doctrine or principles that have general applicability. The partisan fighter is unpredictable and unscrupulous. His weapons are usually simple in design and limited in number. They achieve deadly effectiveness in the hands of a tough, crafty group of individuals who operate almost entirely independent of normal logistical support. Proficient in camouflaging their activities, these men spread a reign of terror over the civilian population of their own country.

Success in antipartisan warfare is not a matter of observing certain rules or applying standing operating procedures that have proved effective in particular instances. Rather, it is contingent upon carefully gathering all facts for evaluating the partisans' command structure, intelligence system, mobility in occupied territories, and relationship to the civilian population. The more examples from practical experience that are available for analyzing these factors, the better prepared will be those who might be called upon to lead the fight against partisans. The study of these examples will condition the future leaders and arouse their imagination, thus preparing them for missions that, under the present conditions of warfare, are likely to be assigned to any military commander.

It is in this spirit that the following small unit actions should be read. Far more important than the application of proper tactics, however, is the adoption of a sound overall policy guaranteeing the successful conduct of antipartisan operations. This policy must develop appropriate propagandistic, economic, and political measures designed to turn the civilian population of occupied areas against the partisans and to obtain its cooperation in the antipartisan struggle. The enforcement of such a policy is the responsibility of the top-level command. It must be planned before the first bomb is released over enemy territory and must be applied when the first soldier sets foot on enemy soil.

During their initial encounters with partisans, combat troops usually tend to underestimate the importance and effectiveness of these irregular forces, principally because their equipment consists solely of small arms. What a dangerous fallacy! In most instances partisans are energetic and relentless men driven by a fanatic belief in their cause. Weak individuals drop from their ranks long before seeing action. The partisans' will to resist and their resolve to inflict damage, regardless of infractions of international conventions, compensate for deficiencies in equipment.

II. The First Encounter (June 1941)

The partisan activity that the Germans encountered immediately after the invasion of Russia was entirely unexpected. German officers who had fought against the Russians in World War I remembered that, when overrun or cut off, the Russians of that day stoically accepted their fate as prisoners of war. In World

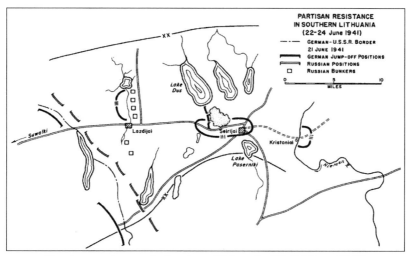

Partisan resistance in Southern Lithuania (22-24 June 1941)

War I it was not unusual for two or three German soldiers on bicycle or horseback to escort as many as 500 Russian prisoners to a distant collecting point.

Small groups of captives were often sent to the rear in the custody of the ranking prisoner. Independent operations by isolated or bypassed groups were practically unknown.

In relying on their experiences from World War I, the Germans overlooked the fact that the Russian Army of 1941 was not a mere continuation of the armies of the Czars, but rather a force born of a long and bitter revolutionary struggle in which the end justified any means. Since the time of the Russian civil wars the partisan fighter had become a legendary figure.

It took but a few days to shock the Germans into the realization that the Russian soldier of 1941 followed concepts different from those of his forebears of World War I.

The Germans learned that isolated Russian soldiers considered it their duty not only to continue the struggle as partisans but also to enlist civilians in their cause. If an isolated group had an energetic leader, its fighting spirit would be rekindled immediately after the initial shock, and harassing action behind the German lines would invariably follow.

The Germans met strong partisan resistance on the very first day of the Russian campaign.

At 0305 on 22 June 1941 the German V Corps invaded Russia from the area east and northeast of Suwalki. The spearhead division of the corps was to break through the Russian front in an operation along the Suwalki-Lazdijai-Seirijai road and, to complete the first phase of its offensive, establish a bridgehead across the Niemen River near Kristoniai (see map on previous page).

The Russian border defenses were quickly overrun by the assault division, which then committed two regiments against the newly constructed fortifications near Lazdijai. The regiment on the right wing broke into that town by 1000, pushed through a narrow passage south of Lake Dus, and established a bridgehead across the Niemen by late afternoon. The distance from the line of departure to the bridgehead was 40 miles by air. The regiment on the left did not penetrate the bunker defenses in its area until the next day.

On the evening of the 22d the division was spread out over a wide area. The leading regiment, together with the reconnaissance battalion and most of the divisional artillery, was astride the Niemen. One regiment was tied down north of Lazdijai, and the reserve regiment, which had followed the lead regiment, was at the outskirts of Seirijai. By dark the entire division area was quiet.

About 2200 the firing of small arms was heard, but neither from the bridgehead nor from the Lazdijai area. It came from Seirijai, the area of the reserve regiment.

At the division command post it was first believed that, in the excitement of the first day of battle, German units were firing on each other in the dark. Soon, however, division headquarters was informed that elements of a German bridge column had been ambushed near the forest west of Seirijai and that traffic west of Seirijai was blocked. A short time later the reserve regiment reported street fighting against armed civilians in

Seirijai.

This report was at first doubted. Until 1939 the area had been part of Lithuania, and its transfer to the USSR under a GermanRussian agreement was strongly opposed by the local population. It appeared incredible that Lithuanians should suddenly have taken up the Russian cause. There was more likelihood that isolated Russian soldiers were continuing to offer resistance. About midnight, nevertheless, the commander of the reserve regiment reported intermittent fire from the forest and stated that armed civilians were actually participating in the fighting.

The regimental commander was ordered to flush the forest at dawn on the 23d. On the assumption that the force in the forest numbered only stragglers and lightly armed civilians, regiment assigned but one battalion to the mission. Following the same line of thought, the battalion commander felt that one company with the support of a heavy machinegun section would be adequate.

After proceeding a short distance into the forest, the company met strong resistance and had to go over to the defensive. A second company was committed without improving the situation. The third company also bogged down, and the operation ended in failure. This failure did clarify the situation. It showed that the force in the forest had been greatly underestimated.

The Russians had achieved a success greater than they probably realized. From the forest they were able to dominate a large area. No bypass around it, protected from Russian observation, was available to the German vehicles, and consequently communications within the division area were interrupted and supplies to the bridgehead regiment beyond the Niemen were cut off. The reserve regiment, one-third of the division's fighting power, was tied down. To solve this serious situation, division ordered the entire reserve regiment plus one artillery battalion committed against the forest stronghold on the 24th.

The attack plan was to destroy systematically the forest force, sector by sector, after breaking the enemy resistance with artillery and heavy weapons fire. For the assault proper two infantry battalions were echeloned in depth, elements of the third battalion sealed off the edge of the forest, and the remaining troops' of the third battalion remained in Seirijai, which was without defense from the south and north.

The attacking battalions met stubborn resistance. A concentration of heavy weapons, mortars, and artillery within the dense woods was difficult and their fire did not always attain the desired effect. Not until the regiment moved its 37-mm. antitank guns to point-blank range were the first partisans overcome. Because it was necessary to use these time-consuming tactics, the forest was not in German hands until evening.

After the fighting was over, the Germans found that some 400 to 500 Russian soldiers, cut off by the German break-through, had formed the nucleus of the forest force. The majority of the force, however, were Russian civilians who had settled in the area after the USSR occupied Lithuania. Some civilians had joined the partisans voluntarily, others under duress. Most of the Russian soldiers had discarded their uniforms and obtained civilian clothing.

The entire force was under the command of a Russian field grade officer who had also organized the ambush in the town of Seirijai. It was estimated that about one-fourth of the partisan force, including the commander, had escaped. Some must have made their way across the Niemen, because subsequently several German officers and men disappeared without a trace as the division continued its eastward advance. In one such instance a German field grade officer vanished shortly after leaving the division command post. In spite of a thorough investigation, nothing was ever found of the officer, his driver, or his vehicle.

The principal lessons learned by the Germans in their first encounter with partisans in Russia, were:

Partisans give no quarter and it is therefore a mistake to employ second-rate or weak forces against them. If casualties are to be held to a minimum and time is to be saved, the antipartisan forces must be as strong as possible and equipped with weapons, such as tanks and guns, that are not available to the partisans.

In order to encircle partisan forces, a tight ring must be thrown around the entire area. Russian partisans did not continue a hopeless engagement, but attempted to disperse, to disappear individually from a pocket, or, if necessary, to break out, and reassemble in a previously designated area. If partisan elements slip through a cordon too weakly manned, they are certain to resume operations in another location after a short while.

III. The Forest Camp (December 1942)

During the winter of 1941-42 the railway line and highway connecting Gomel with Bryansk constituted the principal arteries over which an important sector of the German central front received its supplies. In the vast swampy forests west of Bryansk the Germans were never able to subdue the partisans for any length of time. The partisan forces were much too strong, and their combat losses were quickly replaced by local manpower. They were well equipped with automatic weapons and ammunition from the supply dumps that the Russians had been forced to abandon during their hasty retreat in the summer of 1941.

Under the direct control and close supervision of Moscow, the partisan forces in the Bryansk area coordinated their activities with the operations of the regular Russian forces. The orders of the partisan leaders were obeyed implicitly by the inhabitants of the many remote villages where German patrols were seen only on rare occasions. Over a period of several months the Germans heard of only one case of noncompliance with a partisan leader's orders. In this instance the mayor of a small village had refused to deliver to the partisans the last cow that was left in his community and offered to substitute some sheep. A few days later he appeared at the nearest German outpost, accompanied by his wife and children. He counted out 20 Czarist gold rubles and asked that he and his family be immediately evacuated by air because they feared for their lives. He requested air transportation because he believed that partisan attacks made rail travel too hazardous.

In the summer of 1942 partisan attacks on the railway and highway west of Bryansk were executed by Force Ruda, so designated by the Germans because the village of Ruda was near its center of operation. This force was an extremely active group of 300 to 400 partisans under a particularly efficient and audacious leader who commanded the respect of his men and imposed strK discipline. In the course of time he acquired a reputation as a local hero.

Several German attempts to eliminate Force Ruda failed because the partisans were always able to vanish into the forests and swamps. Early in the autumn of 1942 the actual hideout of the group was discovered—a fortified camp deep in the forest, surrounded by several swamp belts. When the Germans attempted to take the camp their vehicles bogged down in the first swamp, and Major Stein, the German battalion commander, unwilling to proceed without heavy weapons support, decided to withdraw.

The intervening muddy period hindered both the Germans and the partisan forces. Stein used the time to organize five ski companies into an antipartisan battalion. Companies A, B, C, and D were rifle companies, each equipped to fight independently. Each company had 12 light machine guns, 3 heavy machine guns, 6 medium mortars which were transported

A German firing squad executing six partisans in the Soviet Union.

on hand-drawn akjas [Ed: A Finnish boat-type sled], and a number of machine pistols. Company E, the heavy weapons company, had four 75-mm. mountain artillery guns and six Russian heavy mortars. The artillery and mortars were carried on horse-drawn sleds, as was the ammunition. The battalion was equipped with several radio sets.

When the first heavy snows fell in November, the battalion was used to protect the rail line. Because of their greater mobility, the ski units had a decided advantage over the partisans, who made their attacks on foot. On several occasions the ski troops were able to overtake partisan groups that had staged raids against trains.

The partisans, however, were not long in taking appropriate countermeasures. Whenever a ski company occupied billets in a village, large-scale attacks against the rail traffic in the vicinity of the village would cease, and the partisans would restrict their activity to isolated demolitions by small teams. Obviously an efficient intelligence system functioned between the partisans and the civilian populace. Major Stein, who ordered a thorough

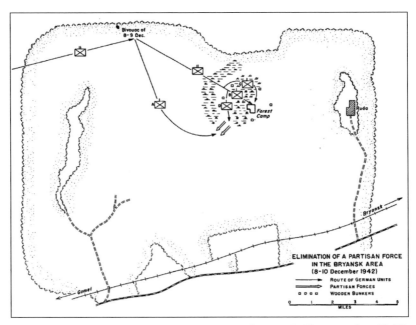

Elimination of a partisan force in the Bryansk area (8-10 December 1942)

search of the villages in the immediate vicinity of the railroad and highway, was amazed at the number of radio sets found there. These were all identical to the model issued to his battalion and must have been taken from German supply trains by the partisans. The recapture of the radio sets failed to produce the slightest effect on the activities of the partisans, who apparently had still other means of communication. Stein then decided to stay out of inhabited localities, even though this meant spending the midwinter nights out in the open. The troops were issued supplementary winter clothing and Russian-type felt boots to be worn at night. By the end of November the newly organized ski battalion became quite accustomed to spending the night in snow huts.

The swamps that had foiled the summer attack on the partisan camp were frozen over by early December. Stein drew up a plan for an attack against the forest camp of Force Ruda.

On 8 December the battalion moved out of its bivouac and entered the forest adjacent to the camp (map above).

Reconnaissance patrols were detailed to observe whether the column was being followed. One after another they picked up four farmers hauling firewood, but found no evidence to justify their suspicion.

When well into the forest the battalion suddenly turned eastward in the direction of the forest camp, which was then approximately 15 miles away. Stein estimated that an attack would be least expected through the desolate swamp area northwest of the camp, and on the evening of 8 December the battalion bivouaced in the forest about 6 miles northwest of the partisan camp.

At dawn on 9 December Company A proceeded into the area just southwest of the camp to establish the camp's exact location. Stein planned to launch the attack on 10 December.

On the afternoon of the 9th Company A reported by radio that a partisan force taking ski training had been sighted at a point presumed to be about 2 miles southwest of the camp. The coordinates of the camp's location were reported around midnight following a reconnaissance mission.

On the basis of the two messages Stein concluded that the approach of Company A had not been observed by the partisans. He was completely surprised when, even before dawn, the company reported that it was engaged in heavy fighting with a partisan force. At 0800 the company sent another report indicating that the intensity of the attack was increasing, and 30 minutes later it radioed that the entire Force Ruda was participating in the action. The company was under intense mortar fire, and partisans were enveloping its right flank. At 0900 the company reported that it was withdrawing westward in a delaying action.

Faced with the necessity of relieving Company A, Stein considered three possible solutions to his problem: the battalion could join forces with Company A, or turn against the partisan camp, or effect a compromise, committing some elements against the camp and sending the rest to the assistance of Company A.

To move the entire battalion to the scene of the fighting was not feasible because Company A was about 3 hours away, and it was doubtful whether the partisans would make a stand since their tactics called for withdrawal whenever faced by superior forces. Even if the partisans did decide to make a stand, the battalion could achieve only a local success at most, and the element of surprise in the main attack against the camp would be lost.

To divide the battalion would be effective only if Company A's commander was correct in his assumption that he was engaging the entire Force Ruda. If this was true, then the partisans were probably holding the camp with few, if any, defense forces, in which case the camp could be quickly occupied and Company A relieved. However, the actual strength of Force Ruda was unknown to the Germans. If the camp was strongly held, splitting up the German forces could only lead to failure of the principal mission.

Stein reasoned that he could achieve a decision only by employing all his forces in one direction, that the main objective of the battalion was the partisan camp, and that, if the bulk of Force Ruda was engaged with Company A, an attack on the camp would divert some of the pressure from that company. Even if the garrison of the camp was stronger than expected, a delay in the attack would offer no greater chance of success than an immediate operation. He therefore decided to concentrate his entire force in a thrust against the partisan camp.

Shortly after 0900 the battalion started its advance toward the camp, Company B in the lead, reinforced by the four mountain artillery guns of Company E. The movement proceeded without incident until 1130 when the forward elements drew submachinegun fire from five wooden bunkers, which constituted the outer defenses of the camp. As the battalion moved forward, the bunkers were evacuated. Company B was about to advance over a second snowcovered swamp when it came under intense machinegun fire from the forest, about 150 yards distant.

Stein ordered Company B to seize the northwest part of the camp; Company C, reinforced by the six heavy mortars of the weapons company, was to attack the camp from the north; Company D was held in reserve. Company A was ordered by radio to go over to the offensive in order to pin down as many partisans as possible. At 1300 Company B approached the immediate vicinity of the camp while Company C fought for the bunkers along the northern perimeter. Shortly thereafter Company D was committed to intercept partisan elements that had broken off the battle with Company A and were attempting to move toward the camp.

Toward 1400, with the aid of the mountain artillery, the last resistance in front of Company B was crushed, and the first elements broke into the camp. The advance of Company B brought relief to Company C, attacking from the north. Company B fought its way to the center of the camp and mopped up the remaining nests of resistance.

By 1500 the struggle was over. Both sides had suffered heavy casualties. Company A lost 25 percent of its strength and was unable to encircle the remnants of Force Ruda, thereby preventing their escape. The partisan leader was killed in Company D's sector. Interrogation of prisoners brought to light the fact that the camp had been held by 150 men, and that a force of about 350 men had attacked Company A. The Germans also learned that the area around the camp, except for a few lanes, was heavily mined. The ski battalion was fortunate in that heavy snowfall had covered the mines, making them ineffective.

The dimensions of the camp and the amount of supplies it contained amazed Stein and his men. In addition to quantities of small arms, there were tons of ammunition and sufficient rations for several months. Moreover, the Germans recovered a great variety of items looted from supply trains, including binoculars, telescopes, and the most recent models of radio sets.

The example shows how an aggressive antipartisan unit, trained and equipped for winter warfare, successfully carried out an operation in forest and swamp over terrain impassable at other seasons of the year.

IV. Attack on a Partisan Headquarters (June 1943)

By early 1943 the partisans were directing their activities mainly against the major railway lines used to move supplies from Germany to the Russian front. Partisan attacks on moving trains and extensive demolition of tracks, bridges, and tunnels at times almost halted traffic on the railway routes Warsaw-Gomel-Bryansk and Minsk-Borisov-Smolensk.

German antipartisan operations had developed a definite pattern. As soon as the location of a partisan force became known, it would be attacked simultaneously from several sides. Dawn was the preferred time for such raids. However, these tactics were successful only if the partisans did not learn beforehand of the Germans' intentions. After Stalingrad, the partisans increased in numbers and improved their organization and intelligence system. More and more frequently the Germans, when closing in on one of their strongholds, would find no partisans at all.

Early in June 1943 the Germans obtained information that the partisan staff planning the attacks against the rail line in the Borisov sector had its headquarters at Daliki, about 10 miles south of Lepel (map opposite). The partisan force at Daliki was no ordinary group, but the nerve center for a large partisan area of operations with a wellorganized system of communication. It was unlikely that the Daliki staff would not learn about a German advance from several sides.

The German commander in charge of the Borisov district

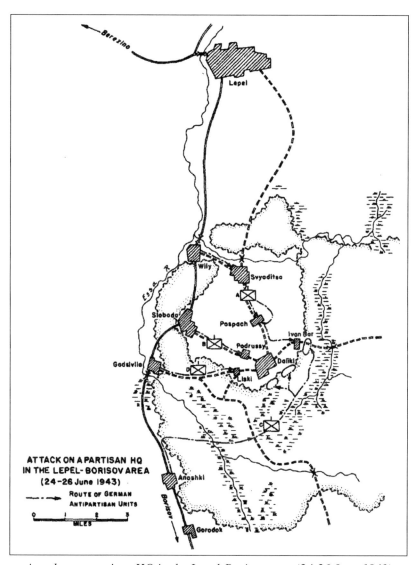

Attack on a partisan HQ in the Lepel-Borisov area (24-26 June 1943)

therefore decided to entrust the destruction of the partisan headquarters to a bicycle-mounted infantry battalion that had been temporarily withdrawn from the front and made available for antipartisan operations. The reinforced battalion consisted of four companies, a headquarters with attached signal platoon, and a motorized supply column; Companies A, B, and C were equipped with bicycles, 12 light machineguns, and 6 light

177

mortars each; Company D, the heavy weapons company, was motorized and had 12 heavy machineguns and six 37-mm. antitank guns.

On 24 June Major Beer, the battalion commander, issued the following order to his subordinates:

"The battalion will carry out an antipartisan operation in the Berezina Valley, 20 miles west of Lepel.

"The battalion, less Company C, will move out at 0700 on 25 June and proceed toward Berezino. On the night of 25 June battalion headquarters and the signal platoon will establish a command post at Wily; Company A will stop in Sloboda; Company B in Gadsivlia; and Company D in Anoshki.

"Billeting parties will precede the march columns. After the units have arrived at their new quarters (about 1600), billeting parties will report to the battalion command post in Wily at 1900 and proceed via Lepel to Berezino where they will obtain billets for 26 June from the local commander.

"At 0700 on 26 June the battalion will assemble just north of Wily and proceed via Lepel to Berezino."

The first day's march went according to plan, and at 0700 on 26 June the battalion crossed the initial point north of Wily and drove on toward Lepel. At the first house on the outskirts of Lepel the battalion executive officer met the column, ordered a 2-hour halt and an issue of rations, and directed the company commanders to report to battalion headquarters at the northern edge of the town.

As the last company commander arrived at the command post, Major Beer stated blunty: "I want you to know right now that I have played a trick on you. Our battalion was never ordered to fight the partisans in the Berezina Valley. That was a fabrication on my part to hide our real objective: a raid on the Borisov area partisan headquarters, reportedly located in Daliki."

The company commanders were not too surprised. If the true objective had been stated in battalion orders, partisan agents would have informed their headquarters in Daliki long before the Germans could have reached the village. Beer continued:

"Let's look at the map. When I was ordered to capture the partisan staff, I tried to develop a plan that would achieve surprise. In this situation I believed that to bring up my four companies during the night and then attempt to break into Daliki from four sides would be impractical. I am convinced that the partisans would have learned of our movement—the distance from Borisov to Daliki incidentally is about 30 miles—and I am even more certain that they would have found out about our assembly at night. We would have found Daliki deserted.

"I would have liked to use a small motorized force of one or, at most, two companies, moving at top speed from Borisov to Sloboda. From there they could have turned right and driven along the cart road to Daliki. The advance elements could have raced right into the center of Daliki, while the rear elements sealed off the village from the south and east, toward the swamp area. That would have been a real surprise! For such an operation, however, we would need cross-country vehicles.

"The solution, therefore, was to simulate a normal march movement, such as is frequently made from Borisov to Lepel, with the partisan center in Berezino as the obvious objective. In order to strengthen the impression of a routine movement, I ordered the battalion to spend last night at a stop-over point on our march route directly opposite Daliki. For the same reason I requisitioned billets in different villages in the usual manner, whereupon the billeting parties were ordered to proceed to Berezino. They are arranging for billets there right now, and not until tonight will they know that their efforts were for nought. All these measures are calculated to prevent the partisan leaders from becoming suspicious, and to induce them to remain in Daliki. I am convinced that they were informed last night that the battalion is moving into the Berezina Valley."

Beer looked at his watch and said:

"It is now 0900. Rest your men until 1100. Nothing must point to the fact that we have a different objective. Until that time our objective continues to be Berezino. At 1100 the battalion will turn around and drive back over the same road we followed this morning, maintaining the same order of march. The three cart roads leading to Daliki will be assigned as follows: Company A will take the road from Wily through Svyaditsa, Company B will turn off at Sloboda, and Company D will take the road from Gadsivlia. Battalion headquarters will proceed with Company D. There will be no intermediate halts, no reconnaissance. The common objective is Daliki.

"I believe that the partisan leaders will try to escape into the swamps south and east of the village. Therefore I have ordered Company C to take up positions at the adjacent edge of the swamp at 1100. Yesterday, as you know, this company remained in place when the battalion moved out and in the afternoon Company C was loaded—without its bicycles—onto six tarpaulin-covered trucks and moved to Gorodok, where it remained overnight. Company C is carrying only small arms such as pistols, carbines, submachineguns, and rifles equipped with silencers [Ed: These were captured Russian rifles that used special ammunition, the report being barely audible at a distance of 100 yards]. Early this morning the company left Gorodok for Lepel. About 1 1/2 miles north of Anoshki, at a point where the forest borders on the road, the column stopped, allowing the personnel to detruck, whereupon the empty trucks were driven on through Lepel to Berezino. My orders to the company commander were to stop for only 30 seconds and keep the motors running."

Beer spread an aerial photograph of the Daliki area on the table and continued:

"Using this photograph as a map, Company C was ordered to march by compass due east through the woods and moors, and, after crossing the Essa River, to advance—or rather wade—

into the swamp southeast of Daliki. It will hide in the middle of the swamp. No patrols will be sent out since the company must remain unnoticed. At 1100, when the battalion turns around, Company C will occupy the fringe of the swamp facing Daliki and a portion of the forest just east of Ivan Bor. However, when the other companies enter Daliki, it will refrain from attacking, its mission being to capture the partisan leaders when they try to escape. Everything else is secondary.

"I would gladly have spared Company C the march through the wet forest and moors, the crossing of the Essa, and the stay in the swamp, where they will be half-devoured by insects. There is a cart road running north toward Liski about 5 miles east of the Borisov-Lepel road, but I believe that this cart road is used as a route of communication between the partisan headquarters and its subordinate units in the forest around Borisov. I have no doubt that an advance along this road would have been reported immediately to partisan headquarters. That is why I ordered Company C to take the more difficult route.

"In my estimate, we shall encounter our first resistance at the farm houses in Liski, Podrussy, Pospach, and Ivan Bor, which form a semicircle around Daliki. I am certain that an important partisan headquarters such as this one would not depend solely on closein security. Any resistance encountered at these farms must be crushed without delay, and for this purpose Company D will detach two antitank guns each to both Companies A and B. At 1200, gentlemen, I want to see you and your companies enter Daliki.

"Are there any questions?"

After asking a few questions the company commanders returned to their respective units in order to brief their platoon leaders. At 1100 the battalion turned around and retraced its route of 3 hours earlier.

At Wily Company A turned off and proceeded through Svyaditsa. The leading elements were almost in Pospach when a machinegun opened fire from there, forcing them to take cover. As the company's antitank guns were being brought up, a second machinegun in Pospach. opened fire. While one, platoon, together with the antitank guns, delivered frontal fire on the partisan machine guns, the two other platoons moved through the woods just east of the village in order to envelop it from the rear. Despite the Germans' attempts at encirclement, the partisans managed to get out, but most of them were cut down as they fled across the open terrain toward Ivan Bor. It was close to 1300 when Company A resumed its advance. Company B, too, was delayed by resistance in Podrussy. Company D was the only one to enter Daliki according to plan.

Company C's platoon nearest Ivan Bor became heavily engaged with the partisans withdrawing from that village. Meanwhile, Company A pushed on, but before reaching Daliki it received an order to turn off toward Ivan Bor and to take it from the west. The company used its entire fire power including 12 machineguns, 6 mortars, and 2 antitank guns, but the partisans in Ivan Bor held out to the last man, very few having been able to get away. It was subsequently learned that when the Germans attacked Pospach, about 20 members of the partisan staff withdrew southward from Daliki and ran up against some Company C men hiding at the edge of the swamp. When asked to surrender, the partisans opened fire with their submachineguns, and in the ensuing hand-to-hand fighting the entire group was killed.

No top-echelon partisan leaders were taken alive. The manner in which they probably met their deaths is suggested by the following account: Soon after the firing around Pospach had started, members of the Company C platoon east of Ivan Bor spotted a horse-drawn carriage coming from the direction of Daliki. In the carriage were the driver and what appeared to be four women, wearing the customary large shawls. Having passed through Ivan Bor, the carriage came to the platoon position.

When the driver was asked to stop, the women suddenly opened fire on the platoon. All five occupants of the carriage were killed in the brief exchange that followed. The four "women" were found to be men—probably the core of the partisan staff However, no documentary proof of this supposition was found.

An attack against the headquarters of a partisan force is always hazardous because a headquarters has a more extensive intelligence system, including closer contact with the local populace, than the ordinary partisan group.

If a large force is, assembled for an attack on a headquarters, it can be expected that the partisans will learn about the impending operation and will avoid an encounter by timely withdrawal. If the unit to carry out the attack is small, its approach may remain unnoticed. Nevertheless, it will lack the strength to overcome even the partisans' security and covering detachments, and will furthermore be unable to seal off the area to prevent the escape of the leaders.

If the leaders of a partisan force are able to escape, the operation must be considered a failure, even if all the other personnel are captured or killed.

A possible solution may be found in the employment of a flexible force organized for swift and effective action. Such a force needs vehicles that can move rapidly over long distances and across difficult terrain. It must have self-propelled guns and sufficient machineguns to knock out security and covering forces, and an assault echelon to raid the headquarters proper and seize the staff personnel. The force should have armored vehicles, flame throwers, mortars, and groundsupport aircraft, and, finally, enough troops to seal off possible escape routes.

In many areas the terrain of European Russia is not suitable for motor vehicles and self-propelled guns. The attack on the partisan headquarters described in the preceding pages occurred in a sector where forests, swamps, and waterways interdicted movements of strong forces. In general, partisans preferred to rely on natural terrain obstacles that could not be surmounted at any season of the year, rather than on customary military security measures.

V. Operation QUARRY (January-March 1944)

The last example of German antipartisan operations indicates the disturbing effect Russian partisans had on the weakened Axis forces in early 1944. Lacking manpower at the front, the Germans were struggling desperately to extinguish the flames of insurrection that threatened their rear area security. Sensing the decline of Germany's military might, the partisans grew ever more audacious. The following story illustrates the desperateness of the struggle.

At the eastern end of the Crimean Peninsula lies Kerch, its white stone houses gleaming in the sun. This city of 50,000 inhabitants, strategically located along the Strait of Kerch, which connects the Black Sea with the Sea of Azov, has had an eventful history since it was founded as a Greek trading post more than 2,000 years ago (map opposite).

After the Germans occupied Kerch in World War II, the city played an important role as a transloading point for shipments to the Kuban area. Early in October 1943, when the German Seventeenth Army evacuated the Kuban bridgehead and withdrew across the Strait because of a Russian advance in the Don area, the city of Kerch was once again in the combat zone.

The Seventeenth Army was composed of German and Romanian divisions. After the retirement from the Kuban bridgehead all but two German divisions and some Romanian units were transferred to Sixth Army, then fighting north of the Sea of Azov. Despite these reinforcements, Sixth Army was unable to halt the Russians westward drive to Kherson, which cut off the Crimea late in October 1943. During the night of 31 October-1 November the Russians carried out an amphibious operation across the Strait and established a beachhead in the

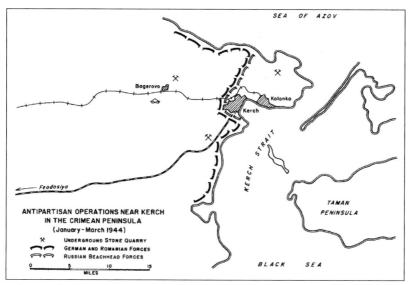

Antipartisan operations near Kerch in the Crimean Peninsula (January-March 1944)

mountainous terrain northeast of the city of Kerch. The German forces opposing the beachhead included the 98th Infantry Division and another division that was brought in by air; Romanian troops meanwhile were protecting the coast on both sides of the beachhead against further landing attempts.

For the next 6 months the Germans succeeded in preventing a Russian breakout. During that time the Russians gradually built up a force of 12 divisions in their lodgment area.

Since the very beginning of the German occupation partisans had operated in the Crimea, although usually only in the woods of the Yaila and Yalta Mountains. During November and December of 1943 the civilian population in the Kerch area caused the Germans no difficulties. Early in 1944, however, this situation changed. Kerch is connected with Feodosiya, a Black Sea port to the southwest, by the only paved road in the area, which was therefore the main supply route feeding the defensive battle around Kerch. The countryside between Kerch and Feodosiya was completely barren; even in the inhabited localities, trees were rare. The monotony of the steppeland was

185

broken only by occasional hills with rocky slopes and naked summits. Visibility was excellent, and thus the villages could be easily kept under control by the German rear area elements. Suddenly a number of attacks on German trucks and personnel carriers took place along a stretch of the road about 3 miles southwest of Kerch. Vehicles were ambushed and set afire; their drivers and passengers killed. Initially the attacks occurred only at night, but before long, officers and soldiers proceeding alone were shot down in broad daylight.

After a short time the attacks spread over a larger area. A German soldier was shot and killed near the Bagerovo airfield, west of Kerch. North of that same airfield a German battalion marching toward the front was engaged by a partisan force that appeared out of nowhere at its front and flanks and then disappeared a few minutes later, as suddenly as it had come.

One afternoon some Romanian troops armed with submachineguns were loaded on a truck covered with a tarpaulin. The truck started out from Kerch for Feodosiya. About 5 miles from Kerch the truck was ambushed, as expected. The Romanian troops returned the fire and, jumping off quickly, pursued the ambush force over the open terrain. Suddenly the Romanians found themselves alone. The fleeing partisans had disappeared as if swallowed up by the ground. A systematic search of the area revealed numerous holes in the ground that looked like shell craters. Closer examination, however, proved that these holes were entrances to a huge underground quarry. Quarries in this region were the source of the stone used to build the white houses in Kerch. When freshly cut this stone was so soft that it could be sawed. Once exposed to the air, it became hard and durable. In the course of 2,000 years the inhabitants of Kerch had worked almost a dozen of these underground quarries, the largest of which had multistoried galleries several hundred yards long, as well as numerous side galleries.

The partisan headquarters was located in a quarry just

southwest of Kerch. Knowing this to be the case, the commander of the Romanian division charged with the defense of the coastal area south of the Russian beachhead decided to wrest the quarry from the partisans as soon as possible and liquidate them in the process.

Should the partisans decide to make a stand, it was recognized that a savage and most unusual struggle would undoubtedly ensue in the dark underground labyrinth. The troops selected for the initial assault—a reinforced company—were therefore issued appropriate equipment. In addition to pistols, submachineguns, flamethrowers, and portable searchlights, they carried large quantities of hand grenades. Two companies were to be held in reserve.

The plan of operation called for all entrances to the quarry to be sealed except one. The assault unit was to use this one entrance, enter the galleries, and overcome the partisans in close combat.

When members of the advance element passed through the entrance, they were sharply silhouetted against the light background and came under heavy fire from the darkness of the quarry. With admirable determination the Romanians advanced about 100 yards into the main gallery and were attempting to break down the resistance in front of them when they were suddenly attacked from the side galleries. Reinforcements were committed but, unable to turn the tide of battle in the underground darkness, the assault troops had to fight their way back to the daylight, leaving behind numerous casualties. The surrendered terms offered to the partisans were rejected. A second attempt by specially trained Romanian assault troops, who entered the quarry simultaneously through several passages, also failed.

The two abortive assaults with their heavy losses led the local command to conclude that the partisans could not be driven but by force; accordingly, all entrances were sealed off in the hope

A meeting of commanders of the Zhitomir Compound guerrilla groups.

of forcing the partisans to surrender through lack of air, food, and water. However, the raids in that area did not cease. One night late in January the troops guarding a sealed entrance were attacked from open terrain. Romanian reserves responded quickly, routing the partisans and capturing some of their wounded.

Interrogation of the prisoners revealed that there were in the quarry about 120 well-armed partisans and a number of women who did the cooking and took care of the sick and wounded. Their leader was an engineer who had been employed in the steel mills located in the vicinity of Kerch. A group of partisans had expressed the wish to comply with the Romanian surrender terms. The engineer, however, had their spokesman shot and established the death penalty for anyone who might harbor such thoughts in the future. The filling-in of the entrances had not cut off the air supply. In fact, this measure proved completely ineffectual, since the partisans had dug new air shafts. During the day these shafts were carefully camouflaged; at night they were used as exits for raids. Food was rationed, but adequate.

There was no real water shortage. A pit filled with water was available and, in addition, dripping water was collected.

On the basis of this information, the Romanian commander asked the Germans for further instructions. To make the correct decision was far from easy. It was, of course, desirable that this partisan stronghold, so close to the German front and astride an important supply line, be quickly and completely liquidated. But it appeared doubtful that a third operation, for which the Romanians requested German aid, would meet with greater success, even if stronger forces were used. Moreover, the Germans were under such heavy pressure from the Russian beachhead that no troops could be made available for the operation and, given a continuation of the Russian attacks, even the Romanian units securing the coast would probably have to be used to help contain the beachhead. Under these circumstances a large-scale operation resulting in heavy losses could not be risked. The Germans therefore ordered that no all-out attack be undertaken, but that the quarry area be completely surrounded by wire. As soon as the wire was in place, the Romanian combat troops were to be withdrawn and replaced with personnel drawn from rear area service troops.

However, the order to set up the wire obstacle was not carried out in full. As soon as the Romanians started building it, the partisans recognized the impending danger and broke through the lightly manned cordon at night, moving bag and baggage to another underground quarry near Bagerovo.

Located 6 miles west of Kerch, Bagerovo with its airfield and railhead was the most important supply point behind the German front in the Crimea. The new partisan base was an even more serious threat than the recently abandoned one southwest of Kerch.

The Germans immediately ordered Romanian units to surround the Bagerovo quarry, an area of approximately 250 acres, and to work around the clock on the construction of a continuous wire obstacle. A Romanian officer was placed in charge of the guard and labor units.

In addition, the Germans provided the Romanian commander with so-called alert units, which were made up of personnel drawn from transportation, signal, and supply units, as well as from kitchens and orderly rooms. One German searchlight battalion was also made available. The force constituted for the main phase of Operation QUARRY was such as was rarely assembled for a combat operation in this isolated theater, where manpower was at a premium. Two Romanian infantry battalions, German and Romanian alert units, two construction battalions, and a searchlight battalion—altogether some 2,000 troops—were tied down by a partisan force hiding underground and numbering little over 100 men.

Within 5 days an effective continuous wire obstacle was constructed. The Romanian infantry battalions and the construction battalions were relieved, and the German and Romanian alert units took over the guard. During daylight hours the number of guards was small. At night, sentries were posted along the wire obstacle and patrols kept the entire area under observation with the aid of searchlights placed on elevations overlooking the quarry.

During the first weeks of their forced isolation the partisans made several attempts to break out at night, but these were frustrated by the machinegun fire of the alert units. Toward the end of February, 3 weeks after the beginning of Operation QUARRY, the first deserters appeared at the wire obstacle. They stated the food stocks were almost exhausted, that contact with the outside had been cut off, and that their leader, the engineer, was preparing for a breakout in order to move to another quarry. On the basis of this information, the alert units were reinforced by two companies.

If the partisans made an escape and succeeded in establishing themselves in another quarry, the Romanian and German forces would have to be spread so thin that there would be no end to this unwelcome diversion. The expected breakout attempt did not take place until late March. Although the partisans displayed their characteristic skill and daring, most of them were killed and the rest taken prisoner. The leader, however, was not among the prisoners or the dead. A Russian radio message subsequently intercepted by the Germans revealed that he had succeeded in slipping through the German lines and had arrived safely within the Russian beachhead. For 3 months he had been the driving force of an operation that had tied down a considerable number of German and Romanian forces and cost them much time and many casualties. Here was an underground operation in the literal sense of the word.

Hunger alone had driven the partisans to attempt the breakout. Had they held out for only a few more days, they would have been liberated, because on 8 April Russian troops pierced the defenses of the Perekop Isthmus and advanced on Simferopol, the Crimean capital. On the night of 9 April the German troops who had contained the Russian beachhead for 6 months were compelled to make a hasty withdrawal across the peninsula.

Although it does not lend itself to generalizations, this example of a force that held out for months in underground quarries is characteristic of Russian partisan warfare. Among other things, it demonstrates that partisans conceal themselves anywhere.

That the initial assaults against the quarry force failed was due in no small measure to the partisans' familiarity with the ramifications of their underground stronghold. This advantage compensated for the numerical superiority of the attack force. Subterranean caves, galleries, and shafts are difficult to locate, and their extension cannot be accurately gaged. It is doubtful whether a third attempt to ferret the partisans out of the first quarry by force would have been successful. The advantages to a defender familiar with every corner of the quarry and accustomed to moving in darkness were too great, particularly in view of the fact that the partisan force had an exceptionally resolute and aggressive leader.

The wire obstacle built around the second quarry at Bagerovo might easily have proven ineffective. The partisans had started to dig an escape tunnel through the soft stone and failed to achieve their objective only because they were physically exhausted from lack of food. The problem of destroying a tenacious force hiding below the surface of the ground other than through starvation, the use of gas, or by suffering excessive casualties among one's own troops thus remained unsolved.

Immediately after Operation QUARRY had been brought to a successful end, the Germans investigated the underground system at Bagerovo and found that it was much larger than the one southwest of Kerch. The Bagerovo system, moreover, was thoroughly organized for a section-by-section defense, principally through the use of built-in demolition charges and machineguns strategically placed to cover the passageways. Every provision for a successful defense had been made; there was a command post with numerous telephone circuits, an aid station, an infirmary, emergency assembly areas, depleted ration and ammunition dumps, a reservoir for collecting drip water, and directional signs in luminous paint. At the beginning of the siege the partisans had at their disposal a small herd of cattle which had been hidden in the caves by local residents. The animals were slaughtered one by one to provide fresh meat. According to local inhabitants, these same quarries had been used during the Russian Civil War in 1917. After the Bolsheviks occupied the Crimea, White Russians were said to have lived in them for years.

PARTISAN COMBAT METHODS

GENERALLY speaking, Russian partisan groups on the Eastern Front were formed early in 1942. At first they were mainly isolated bands of little strength, frequently dropped from aircraft, operating in rear areas well behind the German front. During the summer of 1942, however, these bands were gradually combined into more closely knit groups, put under a unified command: and continuously reinforced. Accordingly, their operations grew in scope and impact.

Partisan group activities seldom covered areas near the front except when extensive, pathless forests favored their approach. In general, the partisan groups would maneuver in the rear areas of the German armies, in woods and swamps next to highways and railroads. They avoided open territory and regions occupied by German troops, but kept the latter under surveillance.

From the outset the German troops had difficulty defending themselves against this type of warfare. Its effectiveness had been underestimated. Apart from the fact that, considering the vast areas, the German forces were not numerous enough to combat the steadily expanding partisan groups, the frontline troops, which had been trained for orthodox warfare, all lacked experience in antipartisan warfare.

During large scale enemy break-throughs, or German withdrawals, strong partisan groups frequently managed to coordinate their operations with those of Soviet cavalry, ski units, infiltrated infantry, or paratroops. Substantial German forces (usually several infantry and panzer divisions) had to be mustered in order to combat the joint enemy efforts. Prior to large-scale Russian offensives, strong bands would often migrate to the areas that the Red Army soon hoped to take. Such movements, therefore, gave some indication of Russian intentions. Prior to the beginning of the large-scale Red Army offensive in East Galicia in July 1944, for example, numerous bands worked their way into the Carpathian Mountains southwest of Lwow, which were among the objectives of the Soviet operations.

On the other hand, during each Russian withdrawal, as well as subsequent to battles of encirclement, innumerable soldiers cut off from their own forces, and sometimes entire combat units, made their way to the partisans and fought with them. In such instances, too, partisan activities developed into a serious threat.

During the winter, strong bands, well organized from a military standpoint and commanded by specially trained leaders, developed intense activity in the extensive woodlands of the Eastern Front.

The bands were generally organized into groupments of from 3,000 to 5,000 men each. As long as the front remained static, these groupments would remain in a fixed location; they were quartered in winter-proofed camps, excellently constructed and heavily guarded. Smaller groups, varying greatly in strength, comprised at least 100 men. Attached to each groupment was a number of these smaller partisan groups. They branched out through the entire rear area and frequently were only in loose liaison with the groupment. They constantly changed their position and therefore were difficult to locate in the vast rear area, which was only sparsely occupied by German troops. They had contact men in all the larger villages of importance to them. Dispersed and cut-off Russian units gave them even tactical striking power. In 1941, for instance, in the area of Army Group Center, 10,000 men under General Kulik operated very skillfully and could not be cornered. Another example was the remnants of the 32d Kazak Division, whose destruction required the commitment of German front-line troops on 6 and 7 August

Soviet partisans defend a Russian village against a German attack.

1941. In 1944, activities of partisans, reinforced by infiltrated troops, had reached such proportions west of the extremely swampy Narva River that the left wing of the northern front (III SS Panzer Corps) had to be pulled back in order to form a shorter and more easily guarded line.

Every camp of the larger partisan groups was secured on all sides—in some sections to a depth of several hundred yards—by thick underbrush, brier obstacles, or abatis and wire entanglements. All roads leading to the camp were blocked or camouflaged, or detours were built which led in another direction. Traffic to the camp was conducted on paths known only to the initiated. Sometimes these paths were protected by bodies of water, with crossings built 8 to 12 inches below water level, or by large stretches of swamp which could be crossed only on swamp skis. All movements of strangers were carefully controlled by sentries stationed far from camp and disguised as peasants. Strangers were also kept under close surveillance by a network of spies active in all villages in the vicinity.

The camps were well supplied with weapons, ammunition, explosives, and rations. Only very reliable partisans were put in charge of these supplies.

The camps procured their food supplies by forced requisitions in nearby villages. Villages refusing food contributions were ruthlessly put to the torch by the partisans; the men were dragged into the woods, and the women and children dispersed. Supplies were also received by aircraft, which dropped the rations in the immediate vicinity of the camp when prearranged light or fire signals were displayed. Looting vehicles during partisan raids likewise provided ammunition and small arms for the bands.

Excellent camouflage prevented any aerial observation of the camps. The shelters were allowed to be heated only at night, so that no smoke would disclose the existence of the camp during the day. The partisans succeeded in maintaining the secrecy of the camps for a long time by having small bands appear in remote villages and by disseminating false rumors concerning partisan movements. The mere suspicion of betrayal was sufficient cause for execution of the suspect. The same fate threatened the family of the condemned. These measures explain why all partisans operations were kept secret. Whoever joined a partisan group, voluntarily or involuntarily, could leave it only at the risk of his life.

The partisans also had signal communications at their disposal. The larger partisan units received their directives by short-wave radio, so that they had up-to-date information about current military developments in their respective sectors. Air couriers were also used. There was a carefully camouflaged landing place for liaison airplanes in the immediate vicinity of almost every major camp.

Practically without exception partisan operations were carried out at night. Daytime raids seldom took place, and then only in areas in which no German troops were stationed for miles around. Raids of that type were usually confined to individual motor vehicles.

A major partisan operation, with the demolition of a railroad bridge as its objective, would proceed as follows: A long column of women and children would move along the right of way in the direction of the bridge. Presuming them to be refugees, the German sentry would take no action. When the head of the column had reached the bridge, heavy surprise fire was directed against the bridgehead from the end of the column. Machine guns, set up on the roadbed in the direction of the bridge, pinned down the German guards. Under this fire cover, and by utilizing women and children in violation of international law, the partisans succeeded in installing prepared demolition charges and in destroying the bridge.

Partisan operations generally included mining main highways, demolition of railroad tracks, mining railroad beds and arming the mines with push and pull igniters, surprise fire attacks on trains, looting derailed railroad cars, raids on trucks and convoys, and burning ration, ammunition, and fuel depots. Less frequent were raids on command posts of higher German headquarters.

The partisans followed the practice of avoiding open combat as much as possible. This practice was indeed the guiding rule upon which their method of warfare was based. Unusual developments at the front would immediately result in extremely lively partisan activity, essentially aimed at the disruption and destruction of railroad lines. During a major German attack, for instance, the main line of a railroad that had to handle the supplies for three German armies was blasted at two thousand points in a single night and so effectively disrupted that all traffic was stalled for several days. Such large-scale operations, carried out by small partisan teams and numerous individuals, at times seriously hampered the supply of the German troops.

DEFENSE AGAINST PARTISAN ACTIVITY

THE German forces in Russia took both passive and active defense measures to protect their rear areas against the surge of partisan activities.

I. Passive Antipartisan Measures

Each army group created a special staff whose duty it was to collect all information concerning the appearance and movement of partisans by close contact with the military authorities in the rear areas and with Russian community heads, as well as by a network of agents in areas threatened by partisans. All information thus gathered would immediately be passed on to the German military authorities concerned.

Small headquarters were combined to protect them more effectively against partisan raids.

Local defense units were drawn from among the Russian population in threatened areas. Often Russian civilians urgently requested this measure because they suffered from confiscation of cattle, forceful removal of men, etc., by the partisans.

All traffic was halted on especially endangered roads at nightfall; such roads were used in daytime only at certain hours and in convoys escorted by armed guards.

Railroads, bridges, and trains were protected. Outguards within sight or earshot of each other were posted along railroad lines in threatened areas. The outguards were quartered in blockhouses protected by wire entanglements and abatis, behind which lay also the entrenchments for defense. Wherever the railroad line led through wooded terrain, all trees within 50 yards of either side of the right-of-way were felled to provide a better

Two Soviet women arrested on a dirt road under surveillance by German police, September 1942

field of vision.

Reinforced outguards equipped with infantry heavy weapons protected all bridges. Another precaution, however, had to be taken in addition to furnishing local protection for bridges and adjacent bridgeheads, particularly whenever larger bridges were to be safeguarded. Strong guard detachments had to be posted at a great enough distance to permit them to spot approaching partisan bands, and to allow time for an orderly preparation of countermeasures. Precautions of that nature had not been taken prior to the previously mentioned partisan operation against the railroad bridge.

All trains going through danger zones had two sand-filled gondola cars coupled in front to protect their locomotives from mines. Each train was escorted by a guard detachment of about forty men.

Furlough trains were guarded by the soldier-passengers themselves. For that reason, all men going on furlough had to carry their small arms. Night traffic on particularly imperiled railroad lines was discontinued from time to time. During the day, the trains on these lines sometimes traveled within sight of each other. This procedure, however, was possible only because Russian air activity in the rear area was very limited.

II. Active Antipartisan Measures

Units such as security divisions and forces particularly organized for that purpose were normally assigned the mission of fighting the partisans. The great depth of area required a substantial number of such units, and since they were not available in desired numbers, security divisions frequently had to be assigned zones that they were hardly able to control.

In the forest terrain of Baranovichi and Minsk, for instance, the German 707th Security Division had to guard an area of 40,000 square miles (larger than all of Austria). It~ duties usually consisted of protection of important points in seriously threatened wooded areas; surveillance and protection of zones and villages through which led military supply routes, and which were constantly imperiled by partisan bands; reconnaissance of partisan camps and roads leading to them; daily dispatch of as many combat patrols as possible into partisan territory to prevent the partisans from uniting into groups and establishing permanent bases; and operations against detected partisan camps.

Whenever the Germans planned a major operation against a detected partisan camp, the project had to be kept a strict secret from the troops. Experience had taught that if such plans were revealed, even larger partisan groups immediately dissolved, only to assemble again at a different location. It happened repeatedly that in carefully prepared operations partisan camps, which shortly before had been fully occupied, were found deserted. The troops, therefore, could only be informed of the actual plans after they had reached the outer line of encirclement.

The assembly of the attacking troops had to take place at least 1 day's march away from the partisan camps. The advance toward the outer line of encirclement had to be so timed that all troops could reach it simultaneously and occupy it immediately. As far as possible, the outer line of encirclement was ' anchored on natural obstacles that were easy to block and to keep under surveillance (for example, rivers). The troops were deployed in the outer line of encirclement in such a manner that they formed a continuous line of sentries, with each soldier within calling distance—and at night, within sight—of the next. Behind this line of sentries, pursuit detachments were kept ready for immediate employment against partisan bands which might break out. As soon as the encirclement had been completed, leaflets were dropped over all inhabited places within the ring, ordering all inhabitants to evacuate at once and to assemble at a designated point.

The contraction of the ring of encirclement proceeded during daytime only, in phases covering not more than 2 to 3 miles per day, and the territory was carefully combed. Individual sectors had to be occupied by at least 2 hours before twilight, so that the troops could establish themselves and become acquainted with the terrain ahead while it was still light.

Sectors easily distinguishable in the woods (glades, paths, railroad lines) were designated as the new line of encirclement. Close contact between individuals had to be maintained. Nighttime security at the sector boundaries was of particular importance. The procedure of detailing forces for guarding unit

A mass execution of Soviet partisans, watched by German soldiers and civilians.

boundaries, as well as the command over those forces, had to be clearly regulated. The further contraction of the ring up to the final encirclement of the camp followed the same pattern as described above.

As soon as the encirclement had started, the surrounded area was kept under constant aerial observation. By dropping messages, the planes immediately notified troops and officers in command of any observed breakout attempts. Since breakouts were to be expected mainly at night, sufficient security detachments had to be posted in front of the sentry line. With the contraction of the ring of encirclement a proportionate number of reserves could be withdrawn, and their follow-up had to be properly regulated. If the partisans still remained in their camp by the time the troops had reached the final line of encirclement, a heavy air attack would usually enable the troops to score a quick success.

Experience had taught the Germans that this type of antipartisan warfare, though requiring large numbers of troops and much time, promised the greatest success. No other methods proved themselves in wooded terrain, since breakouts at night could hardly be prevented. Rigid discipline was a prerequisite for the success of such an operation. The designated objective for the day could not be changed during the operation, and the slightest independent changes on the part of the troops would disrupt the line of encirclement and make the breakout of partisans possible.

Winter proved to be the most favorable season for antipartisan operations because all movements could be more readily observed in snow-covered terrain. In summer the dense foliage of the woods made such operations very difficult. As far as possible they were to be carried out during bright nights, best of all during a full moon. Liberal armament with machine pistols proved advantageous. Mortars were found to have more of a demoralizing than actual effect, since their shells burst in the trees. Artillery could hardly be used during advances in woods. As a rule it could be put into action only during the battle for the fortified camp itself Depending upon the terrain, the Germans found it advisable to have individual guns follow directly behind the leading elements. The employment of tanks, where the terrain was suitable, produced excellent results. In such operations the troops had to have an adequate supply of signal pistols and cartridges. In the case of swampland, the troops were to be equipped with swamp skis.

The wooded terrain, which afforded poor visibility, and deceptions at night often caused shooting frays that started a panic among German units or resulted in their firing on their own troops. The Germans therefore found it advisable to prohibit the firing of all infantry light weapons except during partisan attacks. Special regulations for opening fire also were required when the final ring of encirclement had been closed and the troops were facing each other at a short distance.

NON-RUSSIAN PARTISANS

IN addition to the Russian partisan groups, there also existed in the East strong Ukrainian and Polish groups, as well as a few weak Czech and Jewish groups. The latter two were of no great importance. Some of the bands were for, and others against, Russia. They fought each other cruelly and ruthlessly to the point of annihilation. In 1944, for instance, at the Polish-Ukrainian linguistic frontier, Polish bands raided Ukrainian villages, and Ukrainian bands raided Polish villages, burned them, and massacred the entire populations including women and children. There were insufficient German troops to occupy the entire territory densely enough to prevent such raids. Emergency detachments usually came too late.

Behind the German front, severe fighting, even to ·the extent of employing heavy weapons, frequently broke out between the partisan groups of different camps. Such disturbances at times caused a local paralysis of Soviet partisan activity.

The very active bands of the Ukrainian Nationalist Movement (UPA) formed the strongest partisan group in the East except for the Russian Communist bands, which they fought bitterly. The UPA repeatedly offered its cooperation against the Soviet partisan bands to the German Army and asked for a German general to act as organizer and tactical leader, but the High Command of the German Army, very much to its disadvantage, continually refused these requests. Only tacit, local agreements were therefore made between the UPA and German military authorities. They proved advantageous to both parties. Sometimes the UPA would. participate in fighting the Soviet bands even without any previous agreement (as in 1944 north of Lwow and at Stanislav). The UPA forces were deployed in groups of several thousands each in the rear of the Russian, as well as the German, armies. Although they fought the German political organizations and their police forces, they never fought the German troops, and they seriously harassed the Soviet Army. Not only did they severely impede its supply, they also attacked Russian headquarters and rendered them powerless by encirclement (for example, in 1944 at a Russian corps headquarters in Korosten, which had to be liberated by motorized troops). Furthermore, they incited revolts of the Ukrainian population in the rear area (in Kiev, for example), the quelling of which required the withdrawal of several Russian divisions from the front for an extended period of time.

Although seriously disturbing German supply operations, and thereby also the conduct of battle, even the strongest partisan movement, that of the Soviets, had little influence on the over-all operations in the East. This is illustrated in the report on the protection of supply lines near Kirovograd against partisan raids (1942-43)'.

The Kirovograd region was administered by German civilian authorities, with the aid of municipal and regional commissioners who had their seats in the larger towns. The former town and community boundaries were retained as much as possible. The security of the region was the responsibility of the regional military government officer (Feldkommandant) and the local military government officers (Ortskommandant) under him. It included mainly the security of railroads, the two important supply routes (express highways IV and IVc), and the Bug bridges at Pervomaisk and Voznesensk. Two local defense (Landesschuetzen) battalions were available for these tasks.

'Except for occasional minor sabotage acts against railroads, telephone lines, etc., by the native population, the area administered by German Regional Military Government Office (Feldkommandantur) 509 remained absolutely undisturbed throughout 1942, and substantial progress was made in the work on express highways IV and N c. Not until March of 1943 did a sizable partisan group invade this area.

Of the railroad lines in this region, the one with the branch line to Dnepropetrovsk and Krivoi Rog, via Aleksandriya-Pyatikhatka, was the most vital from the military as well as the war-economy standpoint. The important junction and marshalling center of Znemenka was the point most vulnerable to sabotage operations. Had that place been destroyed, the entire supply of the front, and shipments of badly needed war materials destined for Germany, would have become seriously endangered for a rather long time. The terrain was level and flat, with little vegetation. It was partially steppeland. Except for a fairly large, dense patch of forest between Znemenka and Tsibulnos, only smaller strips of woodland limited the visibility along the railroad line. Features extremely favorable for sabotage operations were the extensive fields of sunflowers, growing taller than a man, and to a lesser degree, the grain fields.

Raids on the railroad line were always carried out in insidiously cunning ways by bands which found refuge mainly in the woods north of Znemenka and which were willingly aided by elements among the population of the neighboring villages. Organized into small combat patrols (Troikas), and carefully protecting their lines of withdrawal, they blew up railroad tracks, damaged control towers and signal installations, and terrorized the native railroad personnel. The Troikas disappeared upon the completion of their work of destruction, as a rule without having suffered any losses. Their activities were directed from a higher level, and they were regularly supplied with weapons, communications equipment, explosives, maps, medical supplies, etc., which sometimes were dropped by aircraft. The explosives consisted of demolition charges, mines, artillery shells, or improvised infernal machines.

The weapons of the Troikas were generally machine pistols, daggers, and rifles. The members wore civilian clothes, but some were dressed in uniforms of the German Army, Luftwaffe, or political organizations.

In March 1943, a partisan group, at first numbering from 200 to 300 men, with a few women as medical and signal personnel, invaded the region of Feldkommandantur 509 at Chigirin (35 miles west of Kremenchug). It was very ably led and highly mobile in its conduct of battle. The group used sleighs in the winter and requisitioned horses during the muddy period. For 3 weeks they roamed through this region; raided agricultural centers, sawmills, and other plants; killed the managers of the agricultural centers as well as the German harvest control officers; liberated prisoners of war; and disrupted rail traffic at Sosnovka. The partisans sought shelter in villages adjacent to woodlands. Horses and vehicles were sheltered in steep ravines to project them against artillery fire. The expertly arranged security and reconnaissance measures precluded the possibility of surprise raids by German troops. Orders and instructions were received by short-wave equipment which was kept in a suitcase. Because of their well-functioning intelligence machinery, searches of woodlands and villages for the smaller sabotage teams of partisans were almost never successful. The Ukrainian community authorities' lists of inhabitants were seldom in order, making identification of the inhabitants of a village very difficult. It was, therefore, found practicable to chalk the names of the residents of each house on the front door. .

In combatting the partisans, railroad stations, control towers, wooded zones, and bridges were focal points of security. Shifting German reserves by motor vehicles was planned for a quick reinforcement of the defenses. All places that had to be defended were converted into strong points. Arrangements had to be made in buildings to permit firing from various floors, and machine gun emplacements with flanking and alternate firing positions had to be installed. Plank walls had to be erected for protection against fragmentation, and windows had to be provided with gun shields and embrasures. Fire steps, ammunition lockers; communication corridors, and observation posts had to be established. Telephone lines were laid so as to be protected as much as possible against gun fire, and supplemented by optic and acoustic alarm signals. In the vicinity of each German strong point, the terrain was cleared of obstructing vegetation for a distance of about 1,000 yards in each direction along the railroad line; this cleared area extended some 300 to 400 yards from the tracks.

The goal of all these precautions and preparations was to assure the smooth functioning of rail traffic. In addition to military security, the railroad lines were frequently inspected by employees walking along the tracks, and patrolled by handcars, or locomotives pushing freight cars ahead of them. The speedy formation of 'alert' units for fire fighting, and the procedure of transporting them by motor or rail had to be planned and practiced in drills. The use of armored trains, or the addition to trains of cars carrying troops, proved to be effective methods of antipartisan defense.

The Germans soon realized that their military forces were not sufficient for the manifold tasks of railroad security. To ease their burden, local inhabitants were assigned to the troops as so-called voice-alarm sentries. Upon spotting partisans, these sentries were to shout the information to their neighboring guard posts, stationed at a distance of five hundred yards, but were not to fight. For that reason the native sentries were unarmed. Their reliability varied, since they feared the cruel reprisals of the partisans against themselves and their families. Organized indigenous forces, some of which were employed for railroad defense, likewise functioned only when they were heavily intermixed with German units. The German regional defense units were not properly armed. Their equipment, too, was completely inadequate. For reconnaissance, the Fieseler-Storch (liaison aircraft) proved equal to all demands. The evacuation of villages directly adjacent to railroad lines, and the establishment of so-called death zones, within which any civilian would be shot on sight, were found to be appropriate measures.